Humans@Work

The official list of contributing authors is as follows (alphabetical by last name):

Michele Fantt Harris
Jill Heineck
Neal Henderson
Mary Pat Knight
Colleen Luzier
Demetria Miles-McDonald
Jeff Nally
Gordon L. Peterson
Lisa Seay
Rusty Steele
Tracy Stuckrath
Shelly Trent

Book typeset by Kevin Williamson
Cover design by Kevin Williamson

Created in the United States of America

23 22 21 20 19 18 17   1 2 3 4 5

ISBN 978-0-9981714-3-2

Note from the Publishers

It's fitting that, for an anthology entitled *Humans@Work,* we had the privilege of joining wonderful humans who provided excellent work. We had a great deal of joy discussing this subject with the authors and reviewing their contributions, and again we feel lucky to be the first (hopefully among many in the HR profession) to benefit from our authors' individual and communal wisdom.

We would also like to thank our network of authors from Red Letter Publishing's Professional Series anthologies, including our most recent titles *Evolution of Human Resources* and *Cultivating Culture.* It's a privilege to remain connected with this growing community as the Professional Series continues to evolve.

Finally, many thanks to Sharon Armstrong of the SAA Trainers and Consultants Network, a free referral service for HR, OD, trainers, coaches, and keynote speakers. Sharon is a HR consultant and author, and she was very helpful to us as we began to develop this anthology. She can be reached at (202) 333-0644 or online at www. trainersandconsultants.net.

— *Cathy Fyock and Kevin Williamson*

Red Letter Publishing and Cathy Fyock are proud to partner with the SHRM Foundation in presenting this Professional Series anthology.

100% of publisher proceeds from Amazon sales of this book will benefit the SHRM Foundation.

The SHRM Foundation is a values-based charity organization whose mission is to champion workforce and workplace transformation by providing research-based HR solutions for challenging inclusion issues facing current and potential employees, scholarships to educate and develop HR professionals to make change happen and opportunities for HR professionals to make a difference in their local communities. Some of the challenging inclusion issues the SHRM Foundation is taking on include: solving aging workforce issues; integrating veterans into the workforce; creating equal gender opportunities; ending employment discrimination; and integrating and engaging individuals with disabilities into the workforce.

The SHRM Foundation prepares HR professionals to take on these challenges by offering scholarships to return to school, participate in developmental seminars and conferences, and obtain SHRM professional certifications. Effective HR practice begins with the knowledge and competency to apply that knowledge. The SHRM Foundation is dedicated to making these educational opportunities open to all HR professionals and students, no matter what life challenges are facing them.

Finally, the SHRM Foundation supports the SHRM chapters and state councils by providing opportunities they can engage in locally to make a difference in their organization and community. Volunteer activities, chapter and programming ideas, fundraising events, and new member recruitment messages are among the resources the SHRM Foundation provides to these groups. All of these resources will focus on inspiring and empowering HR profession to lead transformation that will result in more inclusive organizations that provide opportunities for all types of employees to thrive.

The SHRM Foundation's vision is a world where empowered HR professionals build inclusive organizations where all employees thrive and organizations achieve success.

Contents

Michele Fantt Harris

Selecting and Implementing an HRIS System

NCB's Human Resources department spent a horrendous year trying to implement a new Human Resource Information System. Although we followed SHRM's recommended outsourcing process, there were many "golden nuggets of wisdom" that we learned painfully along the way.

To keep things tidy, I'd like to walk through the SHRM outsourcing process and provide some helpful recommendations for you as you purchase and implement a new HRIS (or any other new system) for your HR department or office.

1. Analyze needs and define goals.

A carefully-planned needs analysis is the first step of the process. Be sure to identify all parties that may be involved in the new system (e.g., Accounting, Information Technology, Compliance, Security, Marketing, Sales, Auditing, etc.). The needs analysis should identify the project goals and expectations of the program. Be sure every department who will be involved with the new system (steering committee) identifies their needs with respect to the system.

Always identify the owner of the system who is accountable for the system's implementation and operation. For example: is the system owned by Human Resources or Information Technology? Have each party or department define their role and identify their needs of the system. Who will be responsible for system configuration and development? Who will be addressing the users' inquiries?

Now that you've determined the needs of the HRIS system, you need to develop a business case to show how the new system will help align Human Resources goals with the organization's business strategy. Show the benefits and the return on investment (ROI) for purchasing and implementing a new HRIS. See the business case attachment for the value of adding a payroll module to a HRIS system.

Develop a charter for the overall project that identifies the goals, objectives, and needs for a HRIS. The charter should also identify how the HRIS will address the organizational goals and strategies, state the project scope, identify the roles and responsibilities of the steering committee members, identify deliverables and their time frames, and develop a communication plan.

2. Define the budget.

Estimate your budget—include the cost of implementation of the system and then each module of the HRIS. What is the budget to maintain the system once it is implemented? There may be a monthly fee per user/employee for the Core module and an additional user fee for compensated and terminated employees. Is there a one-time activation fee? Are there subscription fees (annually, monthly, quarterly)? Remember to budget for consulting and report-writing services with the vendors. It is also helpful to budget for independent consulting fees for outside services.

3. Create a written request for proposal (RFP).

The RFP is a document that requests potential technology suppliers to submit business proposals or bids that address your defined needs and goals for your HRIS. Most RFPs provide an executive summary, company information, deliverables, project/team resources, references, outlined development process, and costs.

Decide what type of technology is needed to meet the needs of Human Resources and your organization. Will you purchase and install hardware and software on user machines that will be supported by your IT department? Will you purchase applications located at the vendor's site that are supported by the vendor's IT personnel? Or will your organization subscribe to software that is developed and deployed remotely and accessed via the Web? Will you use a single integrated technology platform that will support multiple HR functions or will you use multiple systems that support a different HR function?

Be specific for your organization's needs and objectives. Identify the resources needed by the vendor organization.

Ask for references of clients who are currently implementing a new HRIS system with the vendor. Bear in mind that past references may not have the knowledge of the vendor's current capabilities.

Be realistic with your implementation time frame. Remember, Rome was not built in a day. Start with one or not more than two modules—usually payroll and timekeeping—for the first year of implementation and evaluation.

4. Send RFPs to selected contractors.

For HRIS systems, most employers choose a leading payroll vendor or a technology firm that specializes in talent management systems. Research prominent HRIS vendors and select at least five vendors to send your RFP. Give them a specific date to return the RFP to you.

5. Evaluate contractor proposals.

Allow time to receive and for the steering committee members to review the RFP to ensure that their needs were addressed. Review the proposal to see if the vendor can meet the specifications. Is the vendor able to customize the system to address your unique needs? What is the cost of this HRIS in comparison to the other proposals?

Invite each vendor to conduct a presentation to your HRIS steering committee. Ask questions of the vendor to see if the system can address your specific needs and have the vendor demonstrate their system's capability at the presentation meeting. Don't accept any excuses or the generic response our system can do that. Ask the vendor to demonstrate their system's capabilities at the meeting. If they are not able to show you how the system works, don't accept the sales pitch as proof.

Determine if you will have a guaranteed project manager for the implementation and throughout the duration of the project. Ask to interview the project manager prior to selecting the vendor. How long has the project manager been with the company? Are they familiar with different modules within the system? Have your IT and security teams conduct a site visit to the vendor's headquarters and backup data site. Are their backup data centers within the country or at an international location?

In reviewing references, ask the vendor to provide references from current clients of similar size with comparable business processes. Be sure to contact only current employers who are implementing a HRIS at the time of your investigation. Ask questions about the vendor's commitment to quality service and maintaining a state-of-the-art HRIS system.

Here are some vendor reference questions that SHRM recommends:

- How has the system improved HR functions?
- What modules are you using?
- Has the system met your expectations? If not, what is missing from the system?
- Are end users satisfied with the system?
- How has the vendor responded to any problems?

- Has the system provided the expected ROI? Why or why not?
- What was the implementation experience like? Did the vendor deliver on budget and on schedule?

Check the company's reputation in the field of technology. Does the vendor maintain a quality product? How fast has the company grown? A tech company that has grown too fast may not be able to provide a quality product to the users and will not have properly trained employees.

Can the vendor service clients in multiple states within the United States and internationally? Does the vendor keep abreast of the latest employment and tax laws that may affect the employee population of your company? How often is the HRIS system updated with new information?

6. Select a contractor.

After you reviewed all the proposals and saw presentations from the selected HRIS vendors, select the contractor that meets the organization's current and future needs. Do not be fooled by fancy employer awards that the vendor has received; rely on the references of employers who are currently implementing a system. Make sure you speak with companies that have the same needs and are comparable in size and assets to your organization.

If you are anticipating adding a Learning Management System (LMS) to your HRIS system in the future, find out what LMS systems interface with the proposed HRIS system. Conduct a similar review and analyze all potential LMS systems. If your selected HRIS contractor will implement its own LMS module in the future, does the anticipated development time meet your timetable?

Who will help Human Resources and the Information Technology team implement the new HRIS system? Does the vendor provide dedicated instructor services who will come to your location and work with your teams to implement the system? Does the vendor teach your systems project manager and the HR team how to implement the system via webinars and teleconference calls? How does your team learn – auditory, visual or tactical learners? Will the vendor provide a designated manager to see you through the HRIS implementation process?

7. Negotiate a contract.

This step is a negotiation between your legal counsel and the legal counsel of your vendor contractor. This step cannot be rushed, so allow plenty of time for contract negotiations. The contractor's written contract should describe key deliverables, selected software modules, business intelligence reporting tools, implementation time frames, performance standards, testing services, sign-on services, payment terms and fees, proprietary restrictions, auditing standards, insurance, security for program and compliance, applicable laws, confidentiality agreement, training expectations, upgrade costs and responsibilities, and potentially other subjects.

In addition to the standard contract, your company should consider a Nondisclosure and Confidentiality Agreement which sets forth limitations upon the use of information provided to the vendor by your company. The HRIS vendor may have access to confidential employee and dependent data. This agreement says the vendor agrees to hold all "non-public personal information" in confidence. All such confidential information is proprietary and remains the property of your company.

8. Implement the project and monitor the schedule.

Now that the HRIS vendor is selected and the contract signed, you are ready to begin the HRIS project. Select or hire a project manager to lead the initial project planning meeting. Identify the roles and responsibilities of each member on the team. Identify goals and project time schedules.

Effective project management is important to a successful HRIS system implementation. A good project manager is responsible for achieving project objectives with all project resources and completing tasks on a timely basis. The project manager will develop and manage the project schedule, serve as a point person for problem resolution and communicate overall project status and project reporting. It is helpful if the project manager is not the IT systems administrator or the HR subject matter expert, but is capable of guiding the players in all areas of the company to a successful completion of the HRIS system. IT professionals are great, but they understand systems and not people. To have a successful HRIS system implementation, you need the right people, right process, and the right project management.

The project manager should be able to address the triple constraints: Is the project on schedule? Is the project within budget? Will the implemented HRIS project meet the project scope?

9. Evaluate the project.

The last step is the hardest because you are so glad the HRIS system is up and running—so you forget to go back and evaluate the system! First, did the system meet the goals and expectations that were identified in the needs analysis? What is working well in the new system? What are the challenges of the new system? What lessons did we learn from the implementation process? Capture feedback from the employee users about problems that are identified and respond to them in a timely manner.

Taking your time and evaluating each step in the process is the key to a successful HRIS system. In the long run, a well-integrated HRIS system through one or more platforms will be of great benefit to your organization's strategy, your employees' access to pertinent information, and to your HR team's efficient processes.

Payroll Cost Analysis

	TARGET	AREAS BENEFITTED	QUANTITATIVE BENEFITS	QUALITATIVE BENEFITS
1	Vacant positions are currently posted manually using our existing NET system. HR Managers must go to each third party job posting website and manually key each vacant position requirements.	All areas of FIR, Hiring Managers	A HR1S system would eliminate the need for manual entry to each job posting board and would enable the Hiring Managers to upload the data into the HR1S system which each we will not need to manually key any position data. We will merely re-activate the posting.	Once the HR1S system IS populated with all position information for the organization.
2	HR Managers manually review every resume that comes in for all vacancies including non- solicitation and then forward to every Hiring Manager tar them to review the resumes.	HR and Hiring Managers	A MS System would give us the ability to build qualification queries for every vacant position and the system would automatically weed out and forward all resumes meeting the position qualification query to each Hiring Managers	Once the HR1S system IS populated with all position information for the organization. Qualifying candidates resumes would be more quickly identified and forwarded to Hiring Managers immediately.
3	HR Managers await feedback an candidates and who to schedule for interviews via e-mail, verbal phone call and proceed in contacting candidates and scheduling their interviews	HR and Hiring Managers	Hiring Managers would be able provide real time feedback on qualified candidates in the HR1S system resulting in HR Managers being able to schedule interviews in a quicker turnaround time.	Scheduling of interviews would be more timely.
4	[On-Boarding]			

Michele Fantt Harris

SHRM-SCP, SPHR, GPHR

Michele Fantt Harris is the Executive Vice President, Human Resources for the National Cooperative Bank in Washington, DC. A seasoned HR professional, Michele has worked in human resources in education, nonprofit, healthcare and the finance and insurance industries.

This is Michele's fourth professional anthology. To read her previous books, check out *What's Next in Human Resources* (Greyden Press 2015), *Rethinking Human Resources* (Red Letter Publishing 2015) and *Evolution of Human Resources* (Red Letter Publishing 2016).

Active in many human resources organizations, she is a past president of the Human Resources Association of the National Capital Area and the former Black Human Resources Network. A member of the Society for Human Resource Management since 1985, she served on the Society for Human Resource Management national board from 1996 through 2001 and is a past chair of the SHRM Foundation Board of Directors.

Michele is an Associate Certified Coach (ACC) through the International Coach Federation and a Certified Career Management Coach (CCMC) through The Academies, Inc. A member of Delta Sigma Theta Sorority, Inc., she served on the board of the Delta Research and Educational Foundation from 2008 to 2014. Michele currently serves on the board of the Children's STEM Academies of Washington, DC.

She received her bachelor of arts degree from the University of Maryland, a master of administrative science from Johns Hopkins University, and her juris doctorate from the University Of Baltimore School of Law. A certified Senior Professional in Human Resources (SPHR) and Global Professional in Human Resources (GPHR), Michele teaches at Prince Georges Community College and Catholic University. Michele is a native of Baltimore, Maryland, and currently resides with her husband in the District of Columbia with their two canine kids.

EMAIL mfharris@ncb.coop
EMAIL michele.harris19@gmail.com
PHONE (404) 418-9157

Jill Heineck

Personnel to Personal:
Why Engagement Matters During Relocation

In a perfect world, companies would *volunteer* to relocate top talent to locations with key positions—cohesively relocating and on-boarding them, without batting an eye. The results would be *tremendous*. Alas, this is not a perfect world, much less my perfect world.

People naturally want to feel connected to something. When a person accepts a job, they are accepting a lot more than just work. They are accepting a team, a culture, and a community. When they feel connected to a company's community one that respects and appreciates them, they feel valued and empowered to meet their full potential. The rubber meets the road when companies recognize that not only do employees want to connect with the company, but also want the company to connect back with them.

How Does Employee Engagement Tie into Relocation and Why Should You Care?

Think about it. What was your last move like? A piece of cake—or stressed to the hilt?

Every move can be stressful. It's important to always remember it's not just moving stuff and to remain connected to the employee. The business of human resources, after all, is about being human, and remembering that the relocation is that of a real person, a life, and loved ones. It deserves special attention, keeping hte employee engaged. But what exactly does *engaged relocation* look like, and what specifically are the benefits?

Characteristics of Engaged Relocation:

- Transparency
- Flexible benefits
- Dedicated points of contact
- Comprehensive communication strategy
- Collaborative messaging

Benefits of Engaged Relocation:

- Employees feel cared for
- Employee inclusion
- More meaningful contributions
- Increased employee happiness (on the job, at home, among family)

When it comes to relocation, eyes roll and expenses quickly add up. Your company probably considers relocation a costly but necessary evil. And it probably hasn't given a second thought to the fact that there are actual humans going through what can be a harrowing process.

Employee relocation hasn't received the attention it deserves. To date, the industry has offered a few standardized options to relocate employees, then crossed their fingers and hoped it satisfies. But relocating the most important asset of your company should not be about fitting a square peg into a round hole; instead, it should be supporting the real needs of your relocating workforce. It shouldn't be a cookie-cutter or transactional process; it needs to be personal, and adjusted to the individual. Throwing money at the problem typically is not the answer not the highest and best use of the company dollar, in most instances (and it rarely aligns with the goal to retain talent).

Relocation encompasses three of the most stressful events in life: moving a household, acclimating to a new community, and starting a new job. This is why it is so important to be transparent and empathetic towards a transferee throughout the process. Lack of company engagement and connection can lead to a lack of focus—and therefore lower productivity during the employee's first few weeks, or even months, on the job. One study found that law firm associates who relocated without any firm support or engagement spent more than half of each workday managing the move and family distress, which meant slower assimilation into work life and fewer billable hours.

All of this impacts the employee experience. Is the company exceeding their on boarding expectations? If not, many times it leads to an all-too early resignation.

Proactive and Innovative Engagement

By taking a proactive approach through innovative engagement strategies, a company can protect its financial, talent, and mobility investments. Once an employee has accepted the new assignment, companies expect them to be completely engaged in their new role and somehow unencumbered by the logistical challenges of getting to their new location, and getting the family settled in. I can't stress enough how important it is that you have trusted relocation partners who understand your expecations of how to care for your employees during a relocation, your culture, and how the relocation experience impacts them.

According to Nettie Nitzberg, principal at West5 Consulting (a talent development consulting firm based in Boston, MA), in-boarding is just as important for an internal employee beginning a new assignment as on-boarding is for a new hire. Nitzberg—who works with global Fortune 500 companies—says that creating an initiative to "on-" or "in-board" an employee into the culture of their new assignment is a great way to help them acclimate to their new organization or department. This creates engagement from the first day and ensures that the organization sees a return on their talent investment. This—in addition to consistent contact from the hiring manager, Human Resources, and others throughout the move—is essential to a successful transition.

Since mobile families are already anxiously anticipating changes, intuitive companies recognize that front-loaded engagement is necessary for a successful transition. Setting and managing proper expectations *from the start* is one of the keys to the employee's success on a new assignment. A well-designed assignment objective should be known and understood at the beginning of the move. That, coupled with periodic feedback sessions, will ensure those identified objectives are in scope. It's another way to impart feelings of inclusion in the employee while protecting the talent and financial investment of the move.

Electrolux (based in Charlotte, NC) masterfully leveraged relocation for engagement. When they were making the company move from Augusta, GA to Charlotte, they first sent an *invitation* to all 400 employees to join them in Charlotte. Not only was this a brilliant strategic move to give their workforce a feeling of inclusion, it also doubled as an employee engagement opportunity. Employees were flattered to be invited to move with the company; 87% made the move.

In addition, every employee had sufficient time to assess the Charlotte area to be sure it was the right move for them, and each had a buy-out (with a cap) as well as flexible benefits based upon their family dynamic. To top it off, employees had a full year to take a 50% discount on all Electrolux appliances to help furnish their new homes. Do you think employees were talking about this grand gesture with their friends, family, and social media circles? Of course they were! The positive impact on the brand (33% of employees recommend the brand to friends), the continued expansion of the North American headquarters in Charlotte, with the 810 jobs added by 2017 proves the value of their efforts.

The number-one, age-old complaint from relocating employees is that they never knew what was coming next. There were too many people contacting them—or not enough—and the information was never the same. With so many moving parts in a relocation, it is very easy for things to fall through the cracks. By not having a congruent message, provided by appointed contacts along the way, it causes unnecessary stress and confusion for the employee and the family.

Start by managing the employee's expectations from the beginning. Think of relocation as the opportunity to create an unforgettable experience for them and their family. A little goes a long way.

Well-done relocation offers **major** value in the hearts and minds of your employees. Manage expectations early by clearly stating what is available and what is not; remember to under-promise and over-deliver and to send the right empowering message. Your team members should be compassionate and empathetic toward transferees, while working to establish trust. The goal should be closing the gap between *what has been told* and *what is actually being done.*

Ask pointed and poignant questions during the interview process. Refer back to your notes often and address their real issues; let them know how the company plans to accommodate any grievances. Providing this kind of understanding and effort shows the employee that they will be supported by the company throughout the transition. As Nick Saban (head football coach at the University of Alabama) discerned, "One thing about championship teams is that they're resilient. No matter what is thrown at them, no matter how deep the hole, they find a way to bounce back and overcome adversity." Your company's handling of unexpected and exceptional situations can make or break the success of the relocation.

According to a recent Atlas Corporate Relocation Survey, 62% of firms cited spousal/partner employment as the factor that affected employee relocations more frequently. This shouldn't be surprising. Let's face it: if your life partner is miserable, it makes for a miserable transition and a challenging start to your new role. The last thing a working couple needs is for one person to feel as though they aren't important in the move. It seems like common sense: if you are willing to invest in the success of the employee, then by the same token you are required to invest in the success of the family. And this affects companies of all sizes, both domestic and international. After all, the average full domestic relocation costs about $90,000, with international relocation costs sometimes peaking above $400,000. If your company does ten or more relocations per year, or has plans to do so . . . well, you can do the math to see that no company can afford an unsuccessful relocation.

Progressive companies have realized the importance of spousal, partner, or family buy-ins to the move and have responded accordingly. One company (in the hotbed of Houston's oil and gas market) manages two-thirds of its relocations internationally, and found early on that transferees were not lasting long due to trouble integrating – particularly in remote parts of the Middle East. In response, they created an internal community of employees who have essentially "been there and done that," a group of ex-pats who have already experienced the exact move the transferee is about to make. These ex-pats can share tips and tricks on making the move easier by (as one example) providing references for doctors, dentists, schools, shopping, and dining. This community also initiates friendships that have proven to be critical to the success of relocation assignments by creating the much-needed feeling of inclusion. Companies that provide this service to their employees not only protect their investment in the talent move, but also demonstrate to the employee that they give a damn about employee well-being.

The competition for top talent is a motivating factor for many companies to focus on shoring up internal talent. Momentum for talent mobility appears to be building with companies recognizing its mounting relevance in the workplace. What are the risks if an organization lacks a comprehensive engagement strategy? Top talent may disconnect, or worse, resign if they do not see a clear career path.

One global company I know focuses on promotion from within, and they've developed a robust annual career development process. The career development process helps employees continuously grow, learn, and improve throughout their careers. It is more than just promotions or lateral rotations; it is combining the individual's needs with the company's current and future business needs. People grow, learn, and improve best when they are given work that provides challenges within their potential, opportunities to use their strongest skills, opportunities to do what interests them, and chances to be involved in activities that they value and feel a strong sense of commitment toward. Thankfully, the one I remember is not the only company with this attitude. It is becoming a more common mantra among both growing companies and global giants as talent becomes all the more critical to continued growth.

The goal of building strong relocation opportunities is to effectively build a strong culture and environment. It is one of the pillars on which successful companies rest; and by leveraging these opportunities, the company may benefit from further growth and success. However if your company doesn't act in an organized and thoughtful manner, the culture may be lost and the talent gone before he or she ever enters your office. A very specific message should be created to present to those who are being relocated.

Messages like: *"We care about our people and are willing to invest in you."* In turn, that says: *"We care about your career and personal goals, and are committed to help make that happen."* Progressive companies with this mindset are in the driver's seat when it comes to snagging, securing, and retaining top talent.

Let me emphasize that this is not simply about retaining talent. The competitive advantage of magnetic relocation cutlures is that it also *attracts* talent. Remember, disengaged executives from competing companies are eventually going to take a jump—

and they'll start by looking at their company's competitors. So by focusing on creating a positive culture through steps like strategic and planned relocation programs, you will often find yourself as the landing spot for some of the best and brightest.

A significant trend in the talent marketplace today, especially among the fresh-outs and millenials, is how they differentiate and choose their employers. They work just as hard to interview the businesses as the businesses are working to interview them. For top-end talent, it is more of a two-way street than ever before. They know they're good at what they do; they know they are coveted. It's no surprise that they're very particular, that they invest enormous time and energy to ensure that they make the right choice.

Every action, inaction, and decision you make will ultimately become one of the selling points (or repelling points) to prospective talent. Collectively, our goal is to show you how to shift the paradigm and leverage the competitive advantage the marketplace makes available to you. Through this shift, you will find a greater talent retention, as well as an influx of new talent.

Each of these missions place you and your company in perfect position to become a reckoning force in your industry. We all want to be aligned with those who have a great reputation, who are dedicated to the community, and who are always on the brink of growth and innovation. So let's begin discussing a new approach to strategically developing—and mobilizing—talent across the globe.

ABOUT THE AUTHOR
Jill Heineck
SCRP, GMS-T, GPS

Jill Heineck has been the principal of Heineck & Company, Inc. for 19 years.

Jill is arguably one of the most dynamic relocation experts in the industry today. Prior to real estate, Jill worked in sales and marketing for Fidelity Investments in Boston, in addition to running a successful executive fitness, training, and wellness practice. With Jill's creative approach, positive personality, and marketing background, real estate proved to be the perfect way for her to apply her unique talents and an ideal chance to make a positive difference. Since joining Keller Williams Southeast as a founding partner in 1999, Jill has become widely known as the corporate "Relo" expert.

In 2002, she earned her Associate Broker designation, and later earned her Senior Certified Relocation Professional (SCRP®) designation. At the 2012 Worldwide ERC National Relocation Conference, she was awarded the prestigious Meritorious Award, as well as Mobility Magazine's Editorial Achievement Award. In 2013, Jill was awarded the Distinguished Service Award, in recognition of her continuous dedicated service and outstanding professional contributions to the workforce-mobility business community.

Aside from her amazing accomplishments in real estate, Jill has become a requested speaker, moderator, and panelist at HR conferences, and industry relocation conferences. Additionally, she has been quoted in the Atlanta Business Chronicle, Atlanta Journal-Constitution, and The Piedmont Review.

A soon-to-be top-selling author, Jill is working on her first book geared to mobile, global organizations. She wants to inspire companies to use relocation to their advantage.

Jill has been a cancer survivor for more than 10 years—so she understands the importance of timeliness and managing expectations during a life transition.

EMAIL jill@heineckandcompany.com
PHONE (404) 418-9157
WEBSITE HeineckAndCompany.com
LINKEDIN /in/jillheineck
FACEBOOK /HeineckCo
TWITTER @jheineck

Neal Henderson

Tactical Leadership:
Leadership Lessons I Learned as a Marine

Late in my career, I had a lengthy conversation with one of my old bosses. With more than twenty-five years each of Naval service at that point, we agreed that growing into a leader was an extensive undertaking. It requires a combination of in-class studies, reading, and of course, learning from mistakes made while leading others.

In the process of growing into a leader, I have come to appreciate **Kolb's four-stage experiential learning cycle.** In short, Kolb's cycle starts by gaining immediate or concrete experience, which individuals then use to identify trends and specific observations that can be turned into new ideas, pathways, or behaviors during the *abstract conception* stage. Once new processes, behaviors, or ideas have been identified, they can then be actively tested. A cycle like Kolb's is the best way to learn the skills and behaviors of successful leaders. With Kolb's cycle in mind, this chapter examines the leadership principles all leaders need to observe and implement in the foundations of their leadership practice.

Leadership and Management, Tactical and Strategic... What are you talking about?

Language matters. Leading a team can be a daunting task, especially for a new supervisor. When an individual contributor is moved into a supervisor role, many times there's shock as they must hurriedly master new skills and responsibilities. You also realize that leadership language is different; you have to talk a bit differently as a leader.

In today's business and leadership literature, you will see words such as *strategic*, *tactical*, *leadership*, and *management* thrown around – along with countless other terms whose meanings can vary from context to context. To avoid misunderstanding and miscommunication, here are a few useful definitions:

Leadership: the art of influencing others to achieve a common goal or task.

Management: the organization and coordination of the activities necessary to achieve defined objectives.

Management deals with project process challenges such as budget, project scope, and technical details. Admiral Grace Hopper best differentiated leadership and management when she said, "You lead people and you manage things."

Another major difference between leadership and management is the relationships between the leader and the led, as contrasted with the manager's relation to the processes being managed. Unlike processes, people can (and will) say no.

Managers and supervisors perform very different roles. Supervisors observe an employee's performance and provide feedback—so they must have a relationship with that employee. On the other hand, a manager makes decisions about an overall process or action.

So—for example—is promoting or firing an employee a supervisor's role or a manager's role? The processes leading up to the promotion or firing are the supervisor's role, which should be providing feedback and direction to the employee. The decision of whether to promote or fire someone usually belongs to the manager.

Having heard the difference between management and leadership, know this: to truly succeed you must develop and use the skillsets of both. It's worth noting here that Ken Blanchard identifies management as a special *subsection* of leadership.

This chapter is entitled "Tactical Leadership." You might wonder what exactly *tactical leadership* is and what differentiates it from *strategic leadership*, so here are definitions:

> **Strategic Leadership:** Strategic is an adjective, derived from the noun strategy, used to infer a long-term or overarching meaning. The Greeks referred to strategy as "the art of the general." It's considered a long view in a business context, typically meaning more than three years. So strategic leadership is leadership which guides the organization toward the long-term future, helping the organization decide on its long-term goals and aspirations.

> **Tactical Leadership:** Tactical is an adjective. The noun tactics refers to the techniques used to accomplish a task. Consequently, tactical is used to describe a short view, usually dealing with the present; in a business context, that generally means up to three years. Based on a business's strategic plans and goals, tactical objectives are set to achieve the strategic goals. Tactical leadership is the day-to-day team leadership required to achieve the team's assigned tactical goals and/ or tasks.

Another perspective on tactical leadership involves a leader heading a small team (usually 8 to 12 people) responsible for the achievement of assigned tasks. Teams may be comprised of other team leaders, each individually responsible for the achievement of their assigned tasks. To illustrate, the President of the United States leads a team; in fact, he leads several teams. One of his teams is his cabinet, comprised of the various secretaries (Secretary of Defense, Secretary of State, etc.). He will use tactical leadership to get his team to progress toward his strategic goals. Each member of his cabinet team also leads several teams of their own – comprised of the members of their agencies. It can be said the President leads a team comprised of team leaders.

Supervisor, Manager, Leader

In business literature, the term *supervisor* is generally internally focused, whereas *manager* is more externally focused. While a supervisor monitors *people* accomplishing their tasks, they are also establishing an interdependent and interpersonal relationship which influences decision-making. Conversely, a manager is process-focused when making decisions impacting the team. While exploring tactical leadership – the art of influencing a team to achieve assigned tasks – we are exploring the *leading* of a team rather than the *management* of its processes. (Therefore, the term *supervisor* is intentionally used instead of *manager*.)

By observing various organizations of all sizes, many if not most supervisors are well-versed in management roles. However, I believe supervisors need to tap more extensively into their leadership skills. It doesn't matter where a supervisor sits; whether an individual temporarily assigned a couple of people for a single project to the CEO of a large multinational organization, everyone will need to supervise their team direct reports.

As individuals move up in an organization, the strategic-to-tactical leadership ratio will change, but basic tactical leadership skills will always be required. Obviously, a CEO will be implementing more strategic leadership skills and fewer tactical leadership skills than a front-line supervisor, but the basic skills must be mastered at every level.

Reflect on how most of our supervisors *became* supervisors. In many organizations, the only criteria seem to be that the new supervisor was an excellent individual contributor. Very few organizations take into consideration the desire to be a supervisor, the talent development for that person, or what investment in teaching and mentoring will be required for that person to be successful.

Supervisor Roles

Before we can train and develop successful supervisors, we need to review the three critical behaviors a supervisor must regularly execute:

Set Direction and Standards: A supervisor must align team activities to meet the organizational goals assigned to the team, then set their own standards and benchmarks for the task. The supervisor can use these standards to judge whether or not the team has accomplished the designated task. For example, in the Marine Corps I was assigned to oversee a major weekly cleanup of our unit's areas, ensuring the job was done to my Sergeant's standards. One time, I said the job was complete, let my Marines go, then had to take care of all the discrepancies when The Company Gunnery Sergeant decided that job was unsatisfactory. I quickly learned to set my standards higher than my boss's standards.

Remove Barriers: Removing barriers that impede your team requires the supervisor to thoroughly understand organizational goals and aspirations, the task at hand, and the people assigned to accomplish the task. It will also help substantially if you can think three steps ahead of your employees.

Develop the Team: Developing your team will make them excel. To paraphrase Stephen Covey, team development requires building relationships and investing in your members. By using coaching and mentoring skills to apply situational leadership to each individual and to the team as a whole, you will grow every team member's confidence and capabilities.

After discussing these three main roles with new or potential supervisors, someone will always say, "Well, that's great, but how do I *excel* in these roles? I have no clue how to do this in the real world."

There are eleven leadership principles I have adapted from Marine Corps' principles that can be used to excel both as a supervisor, and personally.

11 Leadership Principles

1. Know yourself and seek self-improvement. The bottom line is that a leader must be a continual learner. As the old saying intones, "Once you stop learning, you're dead." It's doubly true for leaders, many of whom miss out on developing their leadership skills. The Marine Corps defines fourteen leadership traits good leaders need to develop to be successful:

- Judgment
- Justice
- Dependability
- Integrity
- Decisiveness
- Tact
- Initiative
- Endurance
- Bearing
- Unselfishness
- Courage
- Knowledge
- Loyalty
- Enthusiasm

Notice only one of these traits—knowledge—has to do with technical skill. Recognizing whether or not you have any of these traits relies upon *self-awareness*, or how much you understand your actions and motivations. Without developing good self-awareness, you cannot be an effective leader; developing self-awareness is critical when dealing with others. You will mature as you progress through your career and experience different challenges. Once you understand things about yourself—like how you communicate, what your personal biases are, and how you like to be acknowledged—your interactions with others will become much more effective.

2. Be technically and tactically proficient. All teams demand that their leaders be competent. In his book *The Five Dysfunctions of a Team,* Peter Lencioni tells us the foundation of a successful team is trust. And teammates will not trust a leader who is incompetent. Competence and proficiency are made up of two factors – the technical and the tactical. *Technical* proficiency is possessing technical skills or "book knowledge." Being *tactically* proficient is being able to use and implement your technical skills. The word *proficient* needs to be emphasized. The Oxford dictionary defines *proficient* as "competent or skilled in doing or using something." A leader doesn't have to be an *expert* in required skills, but they do need to be able to perform them.

3. Know your teammates and look out for their welfare. A leader needs to get to know all teammates. This means understanding not only their professional attributes – such as how they communicate, their developmental level, and their expertise – but also their personal life and motivations. Knowing more about a teammate's life helps a leader be effective on multiple levels. For example, when I was supervising a recruiting office that had to be open from 9AM to 6 PM (at a minimum) but was generally open later, I set up the schedule so that parents would only work on evenings when their kids were not participating in after-school activities. By understanding my recruiters' family lives and what they wanted at home, I was able to incorporate their needs into the schedule. These adjustments made for happier, more productive recruiters.

4. Keep your team informed. This is a very basic function for a leader. Knowledge is power and knowledge is more powerful when shared. Your teammates are inquisitive and want to know what's going on or why things are being done a certain way. The more background and context your teammates have, the better they can provide you with insights and ideas on how to get things accomplished in the most efficient manner. Leaders can lose trust if teammates believe supervisors are withholding information or trying to hide things.

5. Set the example. Be a role model. Your teammates, both junior and senior, will take note of your actions. Be the good example your teammates talk about to others, making sure your teammates can point to you when they are discussing great supervisors. Remember that, when conveying a message, language accounts for only 7% of the message the other person receives—while body language and tone make up the remaining 93%. When you set a good example, you reinforce the messages you want to get across to the team. If you tell your employees that time management is important and you expect people to go home at their scheduled time, think of how powerful your message becomes when you model what you say about work/life balance and actually leave at your scheduled time.

6. Ensure the task is understood, supervised, and accomplished. Think back to a time when your boss gave you an assignment, you brought in the finished product, and it wasn't what they wanted. How did you feel? Probably frustrated or disillusioned. When assigning a task, make sure you and the person doing the task have the same understanding of what's expected. Supervise the process without over-supervising or micromanaging a task, as micromanagement destroys team confidence and innovation. Finally, make sure to follow up until the task has been completed.

7. Train your teammates as a team. To be effective, you need to get your teammates to know each other, understand each other's strengths and weaknesses, and become a social unit that pulls together when working on a task. Tapping into your knowledge of each of your teammates, you need to assign tasks capitalizing on each of their abilities while developing team communication and trust. Building trust among teammates enables innovation rather than dysfunction when the work becomes challenging.

8. Make sound and timely decisions. Nothing frustrates teammates more than their leader not making a decision; they cannot move forward in their work until that decision has been made. No matter the situation, you won't have all the information you want to make a perfect plan, nor will you understand all the consequences in advance. But you must make the best decision you can with the information you have. General Patton once said that an 80% plan executed now will always outperform a 100% plan never executed. When you make a decision and move forward, you can always make a different decision later as the situation dictates. Keep in mind: with more experience and coaching, your decision-making skills will improve in time.

9. Develop a sense of responsibility in your teammates. In other words, help your teammates take ownership in the team. Delegate appropriately and allow your teammates to learn by taking on challenges that enable growth. Delegated responsibilities enable you to concentrate on the development of your teammates while they gain technical capabilities and a strong feeling of contributing to the team's mission success.

10. Employ your team in accordance with their capabilities. This may seem like a no-brainer, but it incorporates both your understanding of your team's capabilities and your understanding of your organization's needs.

11. Take responsibility for your actions. As you're learning your craft, seek out more responsibility and more intense challenges. When you take on new challenges, you will inevitably make mistakes as a result of learning. Take responsibility for these mistakes, and in doing so, you will gain immense trust and loyalty from your teammates.

Putting the 11 Leadership Principles to Work

There's an argument between those who believe leaders are born and those who believe leaders are grown. Personally, I'm in the latter camp. No matter where you are, what stage of life you have reached, or what role you play in your organization, you have opportunities to seek out tactical leadership experiences. Even if you're not at work, you can find the means to take on tactical leadership roles. Volunteer organizations, such as the Boy and Girl Scouts and local youth sports teams, are always looking for new leaders.

The first step in adult learning is to take an action, or terms of Kolb's Learning model, have a *concreate experience*. (For example conduct a meeting) Then you can move on to the most important stage in this journey, *reflective observation*, which doesn't need to be academic or complicated. Rather, it should be very practical. For anyone who has played competitive sports: it should be like watching film of your last game. Take the time to reflect on what actually happened, identify trends and what went well, and discern what areas can be improved; this is the key to successful leadership development. Without completing this stage, the last two stages are immaterial.

Once you have identified trends, tasks done well, and areas in need of improvement, it's time for *abstract conception*. During the abstract conception stage, you will come up with all possible (though not necessarily practical or realistic) options to change your previous behavior/results. Once you have listed a large range of possible solutions, from the very conservative to the extremely outlandish, decide which actions you want to experiment with. *Active experimentation* is the stage where you practice these new skills and behaviors which become the *concrete experiences* for the next cycle of learning.

This journey is not an easy one. It requires you to get feedback from others on your behaviors and actions. Speaking from personal experience, it can be a very hard and humbling experience to get honest feedback—but keep at it. The journey is never complete and the feedback will help you learn and grow.

One last part—not part of the Kolb cycle, but still very necessary—is measuring and celebrating your successes, no matter how big or small.

Unleashing My Leadership

At the end of the day, being a leader is a lot of hard work, requiring leaders to understand themselves as well as their teammates. It is also a continuous learning experience.

The challenge all leaders at all levels face is juggling leadership and management tasks—where good supervisors develop interpersonal relationships to provide feedback, coaching, and mentoring to accomplish day-to-day goals. The better you become at supervising and leading your team, the better your team will perform. And when your team performs well, not only does the organization do well, but your teammates will be the best kind of highly-engaged employees.

ABOUT THE AUTHOR
Neal Henderson
ACC, PMP, SPHR, GPHR, SHRM-SCP

Neal Henderson, founder and President of Front Row Performance Coaching, is an experienced Organizational Development Consultant and Coach based in Northern Virginia. He has spent over 30 years creating successful teams.

A former Navy Master Chief Petty Officer, his extensive public and private sector experience ranges from developing leaders and managers, leading complex change efforts, and increasing human performance. He possesses expertise in Management and Leadership Coaching and Development for individuals and teams, career management/development, and group facilitation.

Neal began his career in the Marine Corps before switching over to the U.S. Navy in 1986, where he reached the position of Master Chief Petty Officer. During his 28 years with the Navy, he taught sales and sales management, and served as HR Advisor to the Commanding Officer of the Atlantic Fleet Career Information Team. Neal also did two tours as a Chief Recruiter, during which time he led over 200 sailors and civilians throughout 4 states and the District of Columbia, and managed the merger of the Active and Reserve recruiting command. After leaving the U.S. Navy, he joined the Department of the Navy to develop and implement human capital policy for the Navy's enlisted forces.

Neal holds a Bachelor of Science in Human Resource Management from the University of Maryland, University College, and a Master of Science in Organizational Development and Knowledge Management from George Mason University.

EMAIL info@frontrowresults.com
PHONE (240) 606-5764
LINKEDIN /in/njhenderson
FACEBOOK /FrontRowResults
TWITTER @FrontRowResults

Mary Pat Knight

The Compassionate Termination

Outside of public speaking, there is little that strikes fear into the hearts of managers more than having to terminate someone. Emotions, opinions, and judgments collide with a sincere desire to protect the company from adverse actions. Add to this any disappointment that the relationship and work product have soured—and finally, heap on looking someone in the eye and saying, "Yes, I am firing you."

You now have the perfect recipe for human disaster.

And that is why it is generally done poorly. We don't know exactly what to say, how to protect the company, and in the middle of all of it are those messy human emotions.

But terminations don't have to be this way. Terminations can be compassionate and dignified, and they can promote good will and self-esteem. They just need to be done a bit differently than you might imagine.

With some attention to *emotional intelligence (EQ)* and *leadership*, you have all the skills in your toolkit to create positive communication even in such trying circumstances. This chapter is a guide to dealing with that management curveball—termination—and how to find your compassion and leadership amid it all.

Why are terminations so difficult to do well?

Any termination, no matter how well-planned and thoughtful, can be fraught with contention and confrontation. They are emotionally draining and deeply stressing events. Poor terminations have several things in common:

1. They appear to come out of left field, with no advance warning.
2. Emotions and judgments take precedence over fact, ,and fear runs the show.
3. The tone of the conversation is tinged with misplaced use of power or authority.
4. The terminator has a bias towards protecting the company rather than respecting the individual.
5. There is a failure to plan the conversation and the steps after it.

6. Human Resources (HR) or Legal runs the show with a robotic script.
7. The root problem is ignored with hopes that it goes away.

Every human being operates inside a comfort zone, usually resorting to what is perceived as normal. People don't want to cause friction. The very nature of termination is a cause for friction—a big request for you and the other to step out of the comfort zone. Faced with a difficult conversation, it's natural to want to hide behind rules, righteousness, rigidity, or false cheer. Human instinct tells us to do anything to hide the vulnerability of having this kind of uncomfortable conversation with someone. We are not wired to want to hurt people—and in fact, we are usually wired to want people to like us. Who is going to like anyone who fires them when those who fire people inadvertently cause hurt?

It's a real pickle.

Additionally, from a communication perspective, very few of us listen with the type of attention that might be required during a termination. We move swiftly toward expressing our point and then quickly move on . . . with even more of our own points. In a termination conversation, listening is *required*—out of respect, but also to avoid exacerbating the situation.

Terminations are viewed as harsh or even as punishment. The goal of coaching and counseling prior to termination is to modify or improve behaviors that don't meet the standards, not to punish the employee. It stands to reason that a termination should not be viewed as a punishment either.

Another reason terminations are so difficult to do well is just pure and unadulterated fear. *What if I say the wrong thing and we get sued? What if the person has a strong reaction? What if they go postal on me? What if I'm just wrong? What if they cry? What if they spread rumors about me or the company?*

Add your own fear here. (You get it.)

What Does a Poor Termination Cost You?

The "distraction factor" alone cuts into productivity. The termination that should have happened last quarter has become a drag on your focus, which impedes your ability to lead. Your team feels it, too. You may think they don't know what's going on, but you couldn't be more mistaken. Teams have a way of finding the drama—and an employee who is on "last legs" makes for easy drama. The team is curiously watching to see how it's handled, how long it will take, and what kind of leader they are working for.

Yes—the terminated employee may create drama. After being fired, it's not uncommon to feel anger toward the company and certain employees within it. If the terminated employee feels unfairly treated, or unheard, you will have trouble. A badly-handled termination could create an emotional explosion that your work teams (and even customers) are likely to witness. The former employee may choose to take private information or even harm the business out of retaliation. In some truly extreme cases, violence happens.

Newer employer-review sites such as Glassdoor are loudspeakers for disgruntled former employees. A poorly-terminated individual now (unlike before) has a public platform from which to denigrate you and your company. If you think Glassdoor reviews aren't powerful, ask any Millennial whom you are interviewing where they got their information about your company. Better yet, be prepared to answer *their* questions based on those reviews.

Possible legal action becomes a very real threat. When the dreaded Equal Employment Opportunity Commission (EEOC) notice or a court summons find its way to your mailbox, all kinds of horrible things begin to happen. You are distracted and worried. Then the issue finds its way up the management chain. Legal bills increase.

Also, there's one other impact on a poor termination that is rarely considered, yet is insidious and real. The backlash happens in the hiring of the replacement. The poor termination decision creates some "emotional backwash" and sometimes that stains the hiring decision—which then happens with resistance, protection, and fear rather than hopeful consideration.

It pays to terminate well.

Why Do They Happen?

Communication and mindset are at the core of poor terminations. Many companies offer surface-level, skill-based training. The much-needed communication training is lacking. The very necessary EQ/mindset coaching is non-existent. The lack of common, basic emotional intelligence hurts our ability to tailor communication to the individual situation. Terminations can become rote, relying on scripting and defense. Now add to that a commitment to positional power rather than personal leadership, and again, you're likely to have a mess on your hands.

Another reason may be that HR is not operating as a partner, but rather, functioning as the legal police for the company—relying on rules and regulations and legal implications, focusing on the paperwork and not the human. These are just a few of the reasons poor terminations occur.

Terminations <u>Can</u> Be Done Well

What does a compassionate termination looks like?

The compassionate termination is a respectful conversation between two individuals that discusses behavioral facts while honoring emotion.

Who benefits when terminations are compassionate?

The person being terminated can leave the situation with their self-esteem intact. This allows him to focus on what needs to be done moving forward, rather than focusing on how poorly the company has treated him. Also, he has security in knowing exactly what next steps there are in terms of money, vacation time, insurance, and unemployment. There is no shame—simply the recognition that this situation didn't work out and the next one is likely to be more suited.

The remaining team is spared drama and finger-pointing. They may have questions and feel the loss of a team member, but they fear less for their own position when termination is done compassionately. They don't have to choose sides between their former teammate and the company. Plus, the leader walks way with his or her integrity intact, and confidence grows in that leader. The conversation has enhanced the ability to be both vulnerable and decisive as a team. There is no need to demonstrate villainous behavior because no person was "wrong"—rather, the behavior choices and the situation created the inevitable outcome.

What is the impact on the business when terminations are humanized and compassionate? Why should you care about letting an employee leave with respect?

Very simple: *employees talk.*

Employees post things on the Internet. Employees talk more. Letting an employee leave with respect makes the final interaction with the company as positive as possible, considering the circumstances. Your organization can live the culture you preach. You can create goodwill in your corporate community. Social media will not be your daily nightmare. In fact, sometimes the bonus is that the compassionately-terminated individual becomes an advocate for the company later (or even returns with enhanced skills and maturity down the road).

Ten Principles of Compassionate Termination

Obstacles and opportunities are first created in the mind. Therefore, these ten principles address both mindset and mindful action. The first and overarching basic principle is that **we are human beings doing the best we can with the information and situation at hand.** When we know more and practice more, we do better. Consider the following principles as guidelines for more than just termination—indeed, they are guidelines for any emotionally-based conversation.

1. Be Present

How you, as the leader, show up will set the tone for the conversation. Being fully present requires that you have become aware of, and cleared up, any strong emotions you might have. Maybe you've talked with a trusted advisor, journaled, or simply found a quiet place to ease your mind. In any case, you show up in the here and now. You cannot predict the future, and the past is already complete. Show up now.

2. Check Assumptions and Judgment

This principle asks you to understand and filter through any assumptions you have made or judgments you have. You are human, so you have them. Being aware of them and neutralizing them allows you to be fair and in control of your own emotional response. The person you are terminating will feel this and his emotions will likely stabilize.

3. The Golden Rule

Simply put, treat people as you would like to be treated. If the shoe were on the other foot, what type of conversation would you want to have? How would you prefer to exit? What emotions might you be feeling that would need honoring? What amount of space would you desire to express your own thoughts and feelings? When you think with the Golden Rule and customize how you communicate, the termination can be done with compassion and dignity.

4. Hold a Safe Place for Strong Reactions

When someone is terminated, it's a kick in the rear, and directly out of an established comfort zone. Those who find themselves here will definitely experience strong emotions, reactions, and defenses. Harsh words, deep emotions, and even some physical responses can all play out. Your job is to create a safe space—after all, you've already done your emotional work around this. This is about supporting the terminated person and allowing them to express and, most importantly, release.

5. Don't Play the Blame Game

The blame game never works. Never. It might provide you some temporary feeling of righteousness or superiority, and it might be a great way to deflect personal responsibility for some things. But it's a losing game. Your employee is likely to point fingers back at other colleagues, the company, or you. Stay in a neutral place. Redirect the conversation back to supporting him and looking toward the future.

6. Support the Terminated Employee's Future

Speaking of futures, all compassionate terminations bear in mind that the person being terminated still has one. When the blame has subsided and the bargaining has completed, the person needs to leave the conversation with some hope for their future. In any way that you can, find something to appreciate about the person and offer hope for the next outcome. There is nothing more devastating than beginning a job search with shattered self-confidence.

7. Do What You Say You're Going to Do

Think out and clearly communicate what you or the company is prepared to do for the individual. Write it out so that the communication is crystal-clear and then **do it**. If you are offering COBRA, make sure the appropriate paperwork is released on time. If you are offering a severance, present the paperwork to be completed with clear instructions, and then pay it as you agreed. If you are offering a neutral reference, provide it immediately. Trust can be built and protected on the way out, too.

8. Balancing Act—Protect the Company, Honor the Person

How many terminations have begun with, "I'm sorry I have to do this"? Too many. Don't say this. When you say this, you dishonor the individual and make the company sound suspect. This isn't about you. You are passing down an appropriate decision based upon business expectations andpast performance-based facts. Be careful of over-offering information or opinions, but balance that protection of the company with appropriate appreciation for the human being.

9. Have You Done Your Job?

Is the employee surprised? Truly surprised? If so, then you have not done your job. Unless there is an egregious act requiring immediate release, no termination should come as a surprise. Your job is to communicate expectations, inspect them, coach and counsel for performance, and make sure the employee is crystal-clear about where their performance falls along the spectrum. This is a balancing act requiring high emotional intelligence as you provide coaching, not criticism. Transparency and congruency are your twin friends.

10. Don't Act Abruptly; Don't Wait Too Long

Timing is everything. If you wait too long to have coaching conversations, they become harsher. Your frustration builds up and spills over. Potentially worsening matters, your employee may have been feeling unsuccessful for too long already. But conversely, if you jump on an issue too soon, it's perceived as micromanagement. In the same way, a termination executed too soon may not have allowed enough course-correction for that employee to become successful, proving only ingyour impatience and urgency. A termination decision that lingers too long has adverse effects on you, your team (by watching underperformance not being addressed), and your business (results falter). Do your investigation, conduct your coaching and course-correcting, and keep open and honest communication. You will know when it's time.

A Plan for Compassionate Termination

Your blame or shame may be telling you that you made a bad choice. You made a mistake. You, or a colleague, is at fault for a poor hiring decision. Here is a little mindset reframe for you:

"This position or place of employment is not a fit for everyone. I don't need to blame or shame anyone. With sincere respect, I now set you free to find the perfect job fit for you. In turn, I now have an opportunity to start fresh and make sure that my hiring plan will find a great fit for me, too."

You can create engagement *even at termination* with this compassionate approach:

Preparation

- *Prepare.* Create a plan and practice your conversation. Write it out if you need to. You should not read a script, but bullet points or pre-scripting is useful to get your head in the right place. The more prepared you are, the more effective the process will be. Finalize all supporting documents and rehearse a script with key messages.
- *Set an appointment.* The right time and place can set the stage. Best practices suggest that earlier in the week is most appropriate. This makes sense for the individual, who will want to move into immediate action to begin their next steps in securing new employment. Never fire on a Friday—and always make sure you have an appropriate, private place for the occasion.

Termination Event

- *Be clear and nonjudgmental.* State the facts. Be direct from the start; in fact, open the conversation with the decision. (If you waffle at the beginning, it will set the tone for bargaining.) Just remember that direct doesn't mean brutal. Be kind but firm. Take a breath after communicating the decision; it needs to sink in for a moment. Again: if you've been clear up to this point, there should be no surprises.
- *Offer a reason.* Make it short and simple; don't drag it on and on. The reason should be a recap of what the employee should already know based upon ongoing feedback and coaching. Use the past tense to keep clear that the decision is final and based upon what has occurred before. Be wary of the canned expression *this just isn't working out for us* or any other crutch phrases. Remember, there is a reason this is happening; most often, that reason is that performance is not meeting expectations. If you have done your job, they will already know this. Lastly: if you find yourself over-explaining, know that this is your discomfort speaking. Recognize those feelings and adjust in the moment.
- *Listen to their point of view.* Whether it changes the outcome or not, allow some space for them to talk. By getting the right mindset, and keeping your head and heart engaged, you can listen without falling into the trap of explaining yourself or defending the decision. There is a reason for the termination and you have briefly and neutrally communicated it. Your employee will have differing or negative feelings and may express them, and you can be strong and compassionate without need for defense. Dignity, respect, and preserving your self-confidence are important. Just listen.
- *Be prepared to repeat key information.* When fear is introduced into a situation, listening skills decline—that's a fact. Your mind scrambles for reasons and then

shoots ahead to thinking about the worst possible outcomes. So your employee may simply stop hearing what you are saying—literally—and you may have to say things more than once for them to sink in.

- *Document.* Ensure that you have documented the termination in a neutral way by focusing on specific behavior, and not their personality or opinions. Remember that this documentation has legal implications. Factual patterned behavior, free from opinions, is the best case. When documenting, remember to include the expected standard of performance and then the behavior that violated that standard. And make sure you check yourself; would you have disciplined other employees for the same problem behavior?

- *Support the individual with outplacement and severance.* Clarify the terms and next steps. Have all the paperwork ready. Not all organizations subscribe to this; still, it's in the best interest of virtually all companies to provide some level of severance. Remember that you are abruptly shutting off this person's financial supply and sending them out into the world—and many people live paycheck-to-paycheck. A terminated employee who doesn't have to worry about the next paycheck is far less likely to give any kind of backlash. Have compassion during the discharge conversation and offer good wishes for their next opportunity. Know that things could get heated or hostile, so be aware of your own triggers. Freely extend empathy, yet don't apologize for your decision. Don't burn bridges.

- *Conclude the meeting.* Thank the person for participating in the conversation. Express hope for the individual. Allow them time to compose themselves. Offer options on how to pack up or retrieve their belongings. We recommend, wherever possible, that employees retain control over when and how they leave that day. That way, they will retain their dignity and be more motivated to speak positively about your company, thus protecting your employer brand.

Post-Termination Event

- *Take care of yourself.* Take the time you need to regroup. This is not an easy task, so be easy with yourself. Reflect on what was successful in the conversation. Debrief what you will do differently the next time. Write notes so that you remember what happened. Sit quietly with yourself for a few moments. You did a good job in a tough situation. For a few minutes alone, this really can be all about you.

- *Take care of the team.* Resist the urge to call a team meeting and make an announcement. Instead, start by personally informing those who need to know and being prepared to communicate next steps, including work-load distribution or new hiring decisions. Your neutral, caring leadership tone will set the mood for the team. Drama-free work zones can result from your leadership.

How many times have you heard a friend or family member express that their termination was, in hindsight, one of the best things that had happened to them? I'd bet more than once. This is a common refrain; it's hard for many such people to recognize it at first, but in the rearview mirror they can see that they were stuck and unhappy. Your compassion might help someone see that this really is the best decision, as painful as it feels in this moment. The key is to execute this plan with compassion, care, and consideration.

Some Final Thoughts

Your thoughtful leadership will set the pace for mindful human interaction at every phase of the employee life cycle. But this is never more needed than at the end of someone's employment. Your EQ will pay off in great dividends.

Emotional intelligence is not a fad that will fade into the management abyss over time. It's a sincere and necessary human skillset. At its very core is the ability to understand that both employee and employer have feelings, and can manage those feelings. Leveraging a whole lot of EQ to customize an appropriate communication, rooted in dignity and respect, that discusses performance and outcomes rather than personality—that's the winning ticket.

Nothing lasts forever—nothing. Learning to let go—and support others to do the same—lies at the heart of compassionate terminations.

Mary Pat Knight

Mary Pat Knight is known as a transformation strategist and is an expert in Emotional Intelligence and Human Resource Leadership. Her 30-plus-year career has spanned marketing, operations, strategic planning, human resources, training, development and executive coaching.

Mary Pat is the Senior Vice President at First Hospitality Group, a leading hotel management firm in the Midwest, responsible for oversight of all engagement, culture and people initiatives for 2000 associates, from HR general efforts to the coaching and training designed to create conscious leaders readied to move vision into action for results.

She is also the founder of Leaders Inspired, providing corporate and executive consultation and mentoring in the areas of Emotional Intelligence and Leadership Development. The 6-part signature series, Leadership Mastery, is a current offering and has become wildly popular due to its interactive team-building style and the undeniable personal and professional results that occur for its participants.

Mary Pat Knight is dedicated to supporting powerful life and business transformation. She helps business owners learn how to express themselves authentically, work from a place of courage and find an inner unshakeable belief in themselves. Her mission is to inspire business transformation and develop solid leadership, remembering that when you are inspired in the workplace, you inspire the world.

EMAIL support@leadersinspired.com
PHONE (312) 834-7259
WEBSITE www.leadersinspired.com
LINKEDIN /in/mpknight

Colleen Luzier

How Do You Let Employees Know They Matter?
Build a Staff Development Program!

How often do we put employee job satisfaction as the first item on our "to do" list? If you're like most people, not very often.

Human capital, however, is your company's most expensive resource (just add up recruitment time and costs, salaries, benefits, and training). Consequently, it makes good business sense to protect your most valuable investment – your people – by engaging them in professional development that is mutually beneficial to them and your company.

Often, companies struggle with how to set aside monies to train and develop ALL their staff. Instead, they focus on investing in their identified "superstars," which can be demoralizing to a majority of employees who are not identified as part of this special group. This can also lead to unnecessary turnover because employees feel there is no future in the company for them. Creating and sustaining a staff development program demonstrates a company's commitment to the growth and development of all staff members.

The Business Case for Staff Development

A staff development program is a multi-faceted, targeted program to promote employee engagement and improve employee retention. According to a recent study by the Society for Human Resources Management (SHRM), replacing an employee can cost your company 30%-50% of that employee's annual salary, and other sources suggest that the cost is closer to six to nine months of the employee's salary. The result of *not* investing in your people is that they will leave your company and you will lose their talent and job knowledge, not to mention spending additional monies to recruit and replace them.

This is especially true for the Gen X through Millennial workers, where the "implied contract" of mutual benefit for loyal service between employer and employee was broken by the boom and bust of the 1980s and the most recent recession from 2008-2011. According to Pew Research Group, Generation X represents workers between the ages of 37-52, and Generation Y, or the Millennials as they are often called, represents workers between the ages of 20-36. Historically, Gen Xers and Millennials have seen their parents lose their jobs—sometimes several times—due to mergers, acquisitions, and economic downturns. For the 20- to 52-year-old worker population, their sense of loyalty is more a question of, "What will you do for me here and now?" A staff development program provides an answer to that question that is beneficial to both employee and employer.

To earn the trust of today's workforce, a staff development program shows employees their employer cares about them and is willing to invest in them. According to the 2015 Annual Training Industry Report, the average company sets aside 5% of their budget for staff training, and this averages out to slightly over $700 per worker. Because $700 cannot realistically go very far, this chapter will concentrate on offering suggestions that utilize internal resources, as well as offering some creative ways to develop staff outside of the organization.

For the remainder of this chapter, **staff development** will refer to any of the following:

- Strengthening employees' skills for their present job;
- Building new skills for employees to prepare them for forecasted skill/job areas;
- Training employees for their new position, including supervisory and managerial positions;
- Developing employees with knowledge of, and even expertise in, different areas of the company, so there is a broad knowledge base as well as flexibility for career growth; and
- Expanding employees' skill set so they are able to grow either within your organization or transfer their skills to another organization. (This may seem counter-intuitive; however, it builds a sense of loyalty and trust with employees when you allow them to grow, whether or not your company is the beneficiary of their new skills. This, in turn, leads to positive relationships and potential employee referrals for job openings, as well as positive feedback on websites like Glassdoor which can help attract new talent to your organization.)

Staff development does not have to be about how many dollars are set aside and made available. It is a matter of using those dollars wisely—as well as investing in the human time it will cost to plan, develop, refine, evaluate, revise, and implement. Even if completely handled in-house without involving outside consultants, or by investing in off-the-shelf training programs, the cost *in human time* to prepare and deliver a staff development program is significant.

The payoff for a staff development program begins to show late in year two and in year three, with staff exhibiting an increased willingness to take risks, providing time-sensitive problem-solving across all levels, and demonstrating loyalty and engagement through lower turnover.

Why Staff Development Matters

We know from the research of Frederick Herzberg that the work environment contains two factors that affect employee retention and job satisfaction: "hygiene factors," also called dissatisfiers, and "motivators." The basic principle Herzberg asserts is that *employment factors either serve as dissatisfiers or as motivators.* If employees are satisfied with their benefits package, then it is a neutral factor; as a neutral factor, it neither causes turnover nor helps retention.

Traditionally, management focuses its efforts on addressing dissatisfiers such as salary, benefits, paid time off, workspace and environment, performance management, and reward systems. These are necessary to be competitive and to attract employees, but they are not "motivators." At its most basic level, Herzberg's research shows that anything that helps an employee stay engaged is a motivator, and that is where the company should focus its efforts for the biggest return on investment. Over the years, many surveys have been completed that have broadened the motivators first identified by Herzberg.

Motivators often include, but are not limited to, the following:

- Feeling "in" on things;
- Being trusted and respected by his/her manager;
- Believing his/her manager has his/her best interests at heart;
- Growing in his/her job in terms of skills and responsibilities;
- Having an opportunity to try new duties without fear of repercussions if he/she fails at his/her new duty, or in implementing his/her idea;
- Being included in decisions that affect his/her work and/or that of his/her team;
- Knowing his/her manager has his/her back (fights for and protects him/her);
- Feeling he/she is valued by management; and
- Understanding what is expected for satisfactory or higher performance.

A staff development program, which addresses many of the points above, can be a major contributor to employee engagement and retention. In short, employees leave companies because the dissatisfiers outweigh the motivators. Conversely, employees stay with employers because they feel included, motivated, and cared about. A staff development program for all levels of staff will increase employee retention, engage and motivate staff, and minimize the loss of key staff that you wish you could have kept.

The Five Parts of Building a Staff Development Program

A staff development program (SDP) is comprised of five stages. Each part must be thoroughly vetted and realistically addressed. The five stages are: Challenge, Culture, Competencies, Commitment, and Continuum. Continuum is the implementation stage and the very last step. Descriptions of each stage are covered in the following pages.

The first four stages of a staff development program need to be completed before rolling out the program. In the final stage, multiple options will be given that will require internal coordination and commitment, but will not require outside involvement unless the company chooses to do that in addition to the internal options suggested.

Realistically, a small task force should be created to research, recommend, and champion a staff development program. The task force should include between 6 and 9 people representing the following functions: human resources/organizational development, sales, each major project or product line, the executive team, and the finance department. The task force should regularly update the executive team on its findings and receive approval for each major milestone prior to moving on to the next milestone. The Task Force should be respected and seen as competent, thorough, and fair throughout the organization, regardless of individual title, level, or department.

Stage 1: Challenge

Any task force considering creating a formalized staff development program should first take a candid, objective look at its workforce. Here are some questions the task force should consider:

- What are the challenges this company is facing right now? Over the next 24-36 months?
- What are our competitors doing to survive? Will a staff development program help differentiate us from our competitors, and how will we know it if it does?
- What is the pace of change in our organization, and will it impede or accelerate the adoption of this program?
- What is on the horizon for our organization (technology, acquisitions, mergers, national or global trends that may impact us), and are we ready for it?
- Is this the right time to expend resources on a staff development program? How and when will we know if it is effective? What are our metrics?
- If we delay creating and implementing a staff development program, what are the potential consequences?

Another area the task force should address during this stage is an understanding of the current state of employee engagement, either through an employee survey or an organizational audit. The employee survey can be short (using a free version of SurveyMonkey, for instance) and focus on staff satisfaction, motivation, desire for training, and level of interest in job/skill growth and career opportunities. Alternately, an organizational audit could be performed that would include an all-employee survey, as well as focus groups and one-on-one interviews with key staff, in order to take the "pulse" of the company at this point in time. Organizational audits usually have a broader and deeper scope, and the staff development program feedback will be one part of the larger findings.

The final component of the Challenge stage is how to identify eligible staff for the staff development program. The matrix below is a simple way to begin to categorize staff. This matrix is a starting point for the SDP, but more consideration for the content of the SDP will be given in Stage 3: Competencies.

When implementing a staff development program, all staff should be eligible for consideration. When identifying which staff members go into which matrix quadrant, do everything possible to validate they are in the correct quadrant. Generally, with the exception of Low Potential/Low Interest staff, all other staff should be part of a staff development program; and for the Low Potential/Low Interest staff, they should be regularly checked on to determine if they now fit into another quadrant.

Stage 2: Culture

Organizational culture is a key component of any staff development program. The task force should candidly assess the culture to determine if it is ready for, and receptive to, a staff development program. If a survey or organizational audit is conducted, feedback on the culture should be part of the assessment. For the best results, a staff development program thrives in a culture of continuous learning and a culture in which failure is considered a learning opportunity, rather than career-limiting or career-ending. It is counter-intuitive to develop a STP in which an employee trying new ways to resolve problems and maintain competitiveness is only rewarded if successful; however, failure results in the person becoming a pariah within the company.

Moreover, there should be a link between staff successfully developing new competencies and a positive performance evaluation. Not every staff development opportunity will result in a promotion or a pay raise, but it should give visibility and recognition to the employee along with incentivizing the employee to continue to stretch outside of their comfort zone.

Finally, the leadership and management teams of the company should continuously build trust and demonstrate a willingness to explore multiple points of view in a straightforward and constructive way. In his book *The Seven Habits of Highly Effective People,* Stephen Covey introduced the concept of Emotional Bank Accounts: every interaction we have with another person is either a deposit (building trust) or a withdrawal (losing trust). On the broadest level, a company's culture should have many more "deposits" and very few "withdrawals" in order to sustain a staff development program that resonates with its employees.

Values are central to any company's culture. If the employee shares the company's values, then those values serve as a motivator: "This is an organization I can believe in." On the other hand, if the employee disagrees with, doesn't believe, or mistrusts some or all of the company's values, then those values serve as a dissatisfier and are constantly undermining the employee's motivations for working there and performing well. Generally, employees "opt out" of working for a company that states values they cannot support. However, sometimes an employee will become disillusioned of the company's values and, at that point, will usually leave the company sooner rather than later.

Stage 3: Competencies

During Stage 3, the task force focuses its efforts on identifying the knowledge, skills, and abilities (KSAs) that are critical to short-term and long-term success, both for the employee and for the company. This means that all job descriptions should be reviewed and updated as needed to align with the current skills, education, and abilities needed to be a competent performer.

Additionally, the task force should be forecasting what future competencies are needed for the company to continue to survive and thrive, and develop methods to grow those competencies. This review of KSAs should be across all organizational departments, staff and line, and across all organizational levels, entry-level to executive. MDuring this process, many companies find that a group of core competencies or KSAs becomes clear.

It is useful to screen for these core KSAs during the interviewing process, as well as cover them in the early stages of on-the-job training to ensure a consistent and level playing field for all employees. Furthermore, buying, building, or utilizing the current HRIS system to track an individual employee's skill sets, as well as to identify relevant staff for different opportunities across the organization, is a useful tool for tracking staff development and engaging staff in areas where they may not be as well known. It also provides a chance for them to expand their knowledge of the company and share their expertise with others.

Taking the time to thoroughly vet the necessary and probable future competency areas will serve the company well as a strategic tool to have the best possible workforce on an ongoing basis. Once you have finished Stage 3, you are ready to move to Stage 5: Continuum (of Development), because Stage 4 should be occurring concurrently with Stages 1-3. Stage 4: Commitment is defined in greater detail below.

Stage 4: Commitment

The most important of the five stages is Stage 4: Commitment. Without it, all the other stages will not be able to function or flourish.

It is critical that a staff development program begins with, and ends with, a **commitment** that starts with the top executive and is reinforced and supported by all subsequent levels below. As discussed earlier in this chapter, a staff development program is a business decision that provides short-, mid-, and long-term benefits to the company. However, it is important that a staff development program begin with the understanding that it will take some time (probably three years) before the benefits will be noticeable, and it may take up to five years before the results seem substantial. Once the program is in place, however, it will pay for itself with reduced turnover, causing a drop in recruitment and on-the-job training time and costs, improved employee engagement, greater productivity, greater comfort in sharing ideas for efficiency improvements, and problem-solving across a broad spectrum of the organization.

As a precaution: it is not enough to start a staff development program with the blessing of the top executive. The top executive and the executive team must fully support and commit to this program and support it throughout all stages, knowing it may be at least three years before they will see meaningful metrics. The executive team should demonstrate ongoing support through verbal and written commitment, holding their managers accountable for showing how they are meeting with and engaging their staff in staff development, and with regular meetings with the task force in order to reinforce and approve each milestone and the next steps. A basic timeline for implementing a staff development program would be:

- Year 1 – Challenge: Do research for informed decision-making; reinforce or begin to change Culture; identify Competencies and build HRIS system; currently build Commitment.
- Year 2 – First quarter: Pilot three or four relevant programs and revise as needed. Second through fourth quarter: roll out programs, trying to hit all levels in first year at least once, with some measures/metrics; continue to reinforce desired culture; revise competencies as needed.

- Year 3 forward: Track metrics; report results; continue executive buy-in; assess staff development program and revamp or eliminate where necessary; rounds of applause!

Stage 5: Continuum (of Development)

When creating a staff development program, it is important to have short-term, mid-term, and long-term developmental opportunities. For some employees, staff development will mean improving their skill(s) for their current job; for others, it will mean developing and learning skills for their next job, or the skills that the task force has identified and forecast as being critical for the company's continued success and survival; and for others still, it will mean training for the job they aspire to, whether it is within their current company or possibly elsewhere.

Even if an employee *does* leave your organization, the odds are very strong that your staff development program kept that employee with you for a longer period of time, and that the employee was more engaged and more productive during that time. Furthermore, the employee will have positive things to say about your company and may directly, or indirectly, help with future recruiting.

To help you get started with a staff development program, this section will describe a variety of development programs that run the gamut from short-term to long-term. Many of the suggestions below do not cost additional training dollars, but do require commitment, time, and coordination. That is why the buy-in from the top down, as well as a supportive culture, are so critical to any staff development program's success.

Short-Term (a few days up to six months):

- Serve on a committee, or task force, within organization to gain a broader understanding of the work other people do in the company and to increase own visibility.
- Send a designee to a meeting in manager's stead so they gain a bigger picture of the organization.
- Cross-train on another job within the same unit, or another unit that the employee is interested in.
- Shadow a person who holds a job or has a skill that the employee is interested in. Shadowing can be for a day, a week, or ongoing over a period of time to see representative "days in the life of." Shadowing can be done in 3-4 hour increments as well, coordinated with the current manager and the shadowed person's manager,

so that an entire day of performing normal job duties is not lost.

- Write a proposal for a new idea, present the business case for it, and prepare a budget. If granted, go to mid-term staff development options.
- Represent the company as a recruiter at a job fair or college campus.

Mid-Term (6-18 months):

- Train/take classes for internal promotion.
- Train/take classes for career path and/or related certification.
- Volunteer outside work, but in a related area, to gain experience in managing and motivating others.
- Join and become involved with a professional association, or perhaps take on a committee chair or leadership position.
- Represent company at professional associations by speaking and/or attending and manning the company booth at professional conferences.
- Job Rotation (can also be long-term): Transfer to another position, perhaps at a lateral level, to learn another aspect of the business. This broadens the employee's knowledge of the company and its work, increases the employee's visibility to other management, prevents boredom or feeling stuck, and helps the company provide short-term coverage for staff shortages in key areas.
- Peer Mentoring Program: This is a nice way to gather employees from multiple areas of the company and encourage them to discuss key career skills and concerns. This can be done as a peer mentoring group that meets monthly, facilitated by a mid-level human resources person, with ground rules that include complete confidentiality. It can also be set up via the HRIS system, matching employees who are interested in learning a skill with someone who has that skill, and the two employees can work out their own mentoring time. This is a very flexible program and can be tailored to your company.
- Stretch Assignment: This may involve transferring to another department or another site, or troubleshooting a really problematic area for the company. It will have high visibility and high risk, and it is therefore important to provide ongoing support for the individual during the stretch assignment.
- Implement and manage an approved new idea for which the company has provided start-up money along with allocated talent.

<u>Long-Term (18 months or longer):</u>

- Traditional Mentoring: This is a formalized program where a more senior-level employee is matched with an employee who is interested in growing their skills, often towards a management role. Confidentiality is a crucial component of any mentoring program, so trust must be established and maintained. Mentors should not be expected to "provide answers" but to ask questions and help the employee walk through alternatives and develop options to workplace situations.
- Job Rotation: This idea was covered under mid-term; however, it could be long-term program depending on the level of the position and the time it takes to understand it well enough to contribute to it.
- Installing a New System: This usually requires working with external vendors as well as multiple internal "customers," and develops a multitude of skills.
- Serve on a charitable board that your company can support in some way (food drives, school backpacks, winter clothing drives, raising awareness/dollars for research, etc.)
- Join or lead a task force to create a new program or policy for the organization, such as a workplace emergency plan.
- Perform a study of a competitor or competitors around certain product or program areas, perform a competitive analysis, and make recommendations to top management.

The above ideas are a sampling of what each company can offer its employees, and which can be handled internally without spending training dollars on an external resource.

Summary

A staff development program engages staff at all levels of the organization to be concerned about, and be able to benefit from, their colleagues' knowledge and skills. It is doable within any organization, regardless of size, and the five stages described here can serve as a blueprint to get you started.

Relevant and helpful resources for you include the Center for Creative Leadership's *Eighty-Eight Assignments for Development in Place*, Beverly Kaye's *Up Is Not the Only Way: A Guide to Developing Workforce Talent* and *Help Them Grow or Watch Them Go: Career Conversations Employees Want to Have,* co-authored with Julie Giulioni.

These are the tip of the iceberg; there is much more out there to help you customize a staff development program for your company's unique work culture and environment.

A staff development program sends the right message to your most valuable resource: your staff. So what are you waiting for? Start developing your business case today for a staff development program that works for your organization!

Colleen Luzier

M.P.A.

Colleen Luzier is the President and Founder of HR Solutions, Inc., which provides customized solutions on an individual, team, Board and/or organization-wide basis to improve interpersonal relationships and maximize engagement.

Prior to starting HR Solutions, Colleen spent eight years in corporate human resources with a national insurance company.

HR Solutions has been in business since 1988. Since that time, Colleen has led the firm in working with a wide variety of private-sector businesses, government agencies, and non-profits to tackle their human-relations challenges together.

Colleen specializes in working with difficult and dysfunctional groups, bringing them to the same table to have real conversations and make true progress. Colleen is certified in the Myers-Briggs Type Indicator as well as the Benchmarks assessment series offered via the Center for Creative Leadership.

Colleen believes that a well-planned, proactive staff development program is crucial for helping employers understand and retain the Generation X and Millennial workforce—which many employers complain they don't understand.

Colleen has served (and continues to serve) on numerous non-profit boards and actively gives back to the community in which she lives. She currently serves on two non-profit Boards—for The Center for Adoption Support and Education and for Hospice Caring.

In her spare time, Colleen enjoys theater, reading, traveling, and scrapbooking. She is married with two grown children.

EMAIL cluzier@hrsolutionsweb.com
WEBSITE www.hrsolutionsweb.com

Demetria Miles-McDonald

Diversity in Business:
A Spotlight on Intersectionality

Put Yourself in Her Shoes

You are a college-educated, African American woman. You've spent the last few weeks looking for the perfect job and finally, an amazing opportunity just became available at a local manufacturing company. You reviewed your resume with a fine-tooth comb to ensure that the important job skills pop out to the hiring manager, and spent hours practicing answers to interview questions you might be asked. You even prepared for some off-the-wall questions, such as "If you were stranded on an island with three things, what would they be?" (Answer: favorite book, dog, and a volleyball.) You've memorized a few company facts and researched some of the business challenges the company currently faces just to prove that you're the perfect person for the job. You've even befriended some of your future coworkers on social media, because this job is *yours*!

The interview day finally arrives. You anxiously drive to the office building. The closer you get, the more butterflies you feel in the pit of your stomach. Your favorite song is on repeat and is giving you the confidence you need to ace the interview. You briefly close your eyes and visualize yourself getting the job. After you pull into the parking lot, you spend a few minutes gathering your thoughts. You take a few deep breaths and make your way into the building. You're immediately greeted by the hiring manager with a firm handshake and a smile, which puts your mind at ease. You feel at home and, sure enough, you ace the interview.

A few anxious days pass as you wait to hear from the hiring manager, who promised to get back to you by the end of the week. You check your email every two minutes until finally, it arrives! You open the email and it reads, "Thank you for taking the time to interview with our company. We were impressed with your skills and experience, but we are moving forward with other candidates. We will keep your résumé on file and contact you if your skills and experience match any open positions."

Your heart falls into your stomach as a wave of disappointment washes over you. *How could this happen?* It felt like the perfect match. The interviewer seemed to really like you; you both reminisced about your college days at the nearby university. It turns out that you both had the same professor for your Introduction to Psychology course. But none of that mattered. You didn't get the job. Maybe they found someone who was a better fit. That's hard to believe, maybe, but it's time to move on.

You meet your friends for dinner and they ask how your job search is going. You explain your lackluster experience and they try their best to console you. One friend even says they recall hearing about a similar experience at the same company, but you pay it no attention.

After dinner, you do some research—just because you're curious—and discover that there are other African-American women who had experiences just like yours, some at the same company. These women detail every step of their interview and then make the outlandish claim that they were discriminated against. You think to yourself: *that can't be true, can it? No way! That's the kind of stuff you hear about on the news, but it doesn't happen here. Could this be more than a coincidence? Could this major manufacturing company have discriminatory hiring practices?"*

After a bit more research, you discover that there aren't *any* African-American women employed at this company. You take this bit of information to your lawyer and he tells you that you might be onto something, that you may actually have a legal case against the company. He investigates further and finds out that the workforce is comprised entirely of white men, white women, and a few African-American men. With virtually no exceptions, the white men are in managerial positions, the white women are in administrative positions, and the African-American men are machine operators. The company has, effectively, segregated its workforce by race and gender.

You and a few other African American women proceed to file a suit. Your claim states that your race and gender were both targets for discrimination—not one or the other, but *both*. Because you're a woman, you weren't hired for the manufacturing positions; because you're African-American, you weren't hired for the administrative positions. A few weeks later, you head to trial.

"You can't double dip," says the judge hearing your case. "You cannot suffer from racial *and* gender discrimination at the same time. Pick one and prove it."

So, you confer with your lawyer to try to determine which type of discrimination you endured. You think to go with racial discrimination. *That's it!* You were discriminated against because you're black.

"Sorry, you can't go with racial discrimination. Black men were employed as machine operators, so they can claim the source of discrimination isn't tied to your race," explains your lawyer.

Then, you decide to go with gender discrimination. Yes, that's it. But your lawyer quickly reminds you that white women are employed in administrative positions, so you can't claim gender as the discriminating factor either.

What do you do? What *can* you do? Legally, you can't prove gender or racial discrimination, but you know it was both. In the end, the judge dismisses your case.

Believe it or not, this really happened. A group of African American women were discriminated against due to their race and gender, but the courts refused to acknowledge it. This case highlighted a gap in the legal system, but it also reflects how most diversity and inclusion programs operate in business.

Intersect-what?

Diversity is on the agenda of every conference and leadership meeting. Leaders ask, "How do we improve diversity? How do we find diverse candidates? How do we increase inclusion?" The list of standard questions is endless, and everyone is looking for answers. Diversity leaders group people into categories in an attempt to try to understand their experiences. So we group people together by race, ethnicity, gender identity, age, disability, and so on. Everyone fits neatly into these categories. Still, notice that we start by trying to simplify identity into a series of checkboxes.

We compare men to women, white people to people of color, and cisgender and straight to LGBTQ. Many leaders discuss solutions that impact these discrete categories; the problem is that these solutions are one-dimensional.

Even the popular lines of research from which diversity solutions are derived lack diversity. For example, there's been a lot of research to dispel the myth that the traits stereotypically assigned to women, such as compassion and kindness, are not the traits necessary to be great leaders. This line of research goes back decades. But when you dig into the demographics of the data sample used to support this research, you realize that the vast majority of the people in the sample are white men and white women. Yet we have taken the results of such research and applied it to women of all races, ages, and sexual orientations. This one-dimensional view of diversity incorrectly assumes that all women experience the world and workplace in the same ways.

Let me suggest that this is the reason why, out of the 29 women who currently hold CEO positions at Fortune 500 companies, only four are women of color.

If leaders really want to solve diversity "problems" in their companies, we have to move past this one-dimensional, siloed analysis of diversity.

We have to talk about **intersectionality.**

Intersectionality is when a person identifies with two or more minority or oppressed groups. The term was coined in 1989 by Kimberle Crenshaw. She assisted the legal team in the revolutionary case of the African American women bringing discrimination charges against the manufacturing company. However, the concept of intersectionality has been around for centuries. (It can be dated back to Sojourner Truth's 1851 "Ain't I a Woman?" speech, if not much further.)

Early research into intersectionality showed that identifying with two or more marginalized groups, such as being an African American woman, meant that one had experiences congruent with being African American and experiences congruent with being a woman. Here's where it gets tricky: what the public grasps about "being African-American" tends more to reflect the experience of African-American males, and what the public grasps about "being a woman" tends more to reflect the experience of white women.

In other words, we've talked this whole time as though **African-American + woman = African-American woman**. However, recent research on intersectionality has illustrated that such an experience is not "mathematical," where the result is predictable based on the equation; rather, intersectionality can best be imagined as a chemical reaction.

Think about the periodic table of elements. (Yes, take it back to your high school chemistry days.) The periodic table of elements is a one-stop glance at each element's number of protons, electrons, and other chemical properties. As you may recall, the elements are organized by their similarities; Column 18 contains the noble gases, for example. The elements have been dissected and studied extensively so that we can better understand how they function in the world.

It's important to understand each of these elements alone. For instance, understanding how oxygen works by itself is great! People need to know how our bodies and plants use oxygen, at least in the most basic ways. But thinking about oxygen only in singularity prevents us from understanding how water, or H_2O, works. The combination of hydrogen and oxygen creates a completely different compound.

Leaders in business need to think about diversity the same way. In the Table of Diversity (found at tableofdiversity.com), the "elements" of diversity are grouped together based on categories such as race, gender identity, and disability. As with chemistry, it is vital for leaders to understand how each of the diversity elements operates on its own, but very few people identify with only one marginalized group.

Humans at work are complicated, multi-dimensional beings. Intersectionality looks at how these identities work together to create a unique experience. Jane, an Asian-American woman with a physical disability, identifies with three marginalized groups:

the Asian-American group, the woman group, and the physical disability group. John, a gay African-American man born in the early 60s identifies with three marginalized groups: the African-American group, the gay group, and the Baby Boomer group. In most circumstances, being a man means that John is in the dominant, least oppressed group.

Jenny, a white woman who dropped out of high school in the 10th grade, identifies with two marginalized groups: the woman group and the "less than a high school diploma" group. Being white, Jenny is often afforded more privileges than people of color and is considered part of the dominant group. Even within identities, different levels of privilege exist. In the African-American community, for example, darker-toned skin is considered inferior to lighter-toned skin. In the Asian community, being single after a certain age can result in being disowned by one's family and culture.

How can leaders successfully increase diversity and improve inclusionary behaviors if we are only focusing on a few categories, and only by themselves?

Intersectional Humans@Work

Employee resource groups are the most common and foundational diversity initiatives in business. If a company wants to improve the conditions for a group of people or wants to solve a business challenge related to this demographic, leaders will start a resource group. The hope is that anyone who identifies with this demographic will come together to share their experiences and recommend a solution.

Seems like a step in the right direction, right? Many organizations have found great success utilizing employee resource groups, but they're not without their flaws. If you *only* identify as Latino or Hispanic, or disabled, or African-American, or LGBTQ, or a woman, or a veteran, then employee resource groups are the perfect solution. It's rarely that simple; yet unfortunately, these are the demographics on which most diversity initiatives focus in order to increase their presence and inclusion. When employee resource groups come together, they talk about topics that are relevant for the least diverse group, which tends to be the demographic most represented. In most cases, this is the group that's closest to the "mythical norm."

The "mythical norm" is a rich, young, thin, highly educated, Christian, heterosexual, married, cisgender, white man with no disabilities and two kids. Each of these traits is dominant in their category, and when combined, create the "ideal" person. This person rarely exists in the workplace, but it is the standard to which all other people are implicitly compared.

The slightest deviation away from this mythical norm results in some shade of oppressive experience. More than one deviation away from the mythical norm creates even greater levels of oppression. For each degree of separation between an employee and the mythical norm, the more complicated his or her experience. An old, thin, rich, heterosexual white man may experience *some* oppression due to his age—but a young, obese, poor, heterosexual black male will experience a significant amount of oppression due to his physical appearance, socioeconomic status, and race. These levels of oppression shape the way people see and navigate the world.

This perspective is the sweet spot for employers looking to attract, retain, and develop diverse talent. As diversity and inclusion programs shift to an intersectional viewpoint, leaders will uncover solutions to their organization's most pressing problems.

One of the biggest dilemmas African-American women face in the workplace is whether to wear their hair in its naturally curly state or to straighten it. Naturally curly hair has stereotypically been viewed as unkempt and unprofessional, so for many years African-American women have straightened their hair to fit into the dominant culture.

However, more African-American women are beginning to embrace their natural hair, in spite of the negative connotations associated with it. It is very unlikely that this will be the topic of conversation at a women's employee resource group because, quite simply, the least diverse group never has to worry about the issue of afros in the workplace. It's only somewhat likely to be the topic of conversation at an African-American employee resource group, even though the latter group is likelier to understand. As a result, this small but sensitive dilemma falls through the cracks. The perspective of the African-American woman is pushed to the side.

If the focus shifted to an intersectional perspective, we could uncover a high level of creativity, confidence, and rebellion in an African-American woman's decision to wear her hair in its natural state. For what anyone knows, her perspective can help organizations identify new markets, rethink societal norms, and attract untapped talent. She is equipped to lead the organization into uncharted territory because of the way she has had to lead her life. It all stems from her intersectional traits.

Ask an African-American woman about her "natural hair journey." She will likely walk you through a timeline of trial and error: sleeping with her hair in a "pineapple," wearing protective styles, and a daily and weekly hair care routine consisting of washing, co-washing, deep conditioning, hair milk, and curl cream, just to name a few. She might also tell you about the anxiety she had the first time she walked into work with her natural hair. She may tell you about the time(s) one of her co-workers touched her hair to find out if it was soft.

It is the responsibility of the leaders in your organization to utilize her experience in their business strategy. If companies continue to focus on diversity from a one--dimensional standpoint, her experiences won't be utilized because the leaders won't even know that it exists. Did you?

So, the first thing business leaders must realize is that "H_2O" exists. Groups identifying with more than one demographic exist and are in need of attention. Once leaders recognize the individuality of each person, recruiting begins to look different. Recruiters seek candidates with several marginalized identities to enrich the culture. Hiring managers understand that the layers a person possesses are not a deterrent but an opportunity to capitalize on a treasure. The interviewer incorporates appropriate questions regarding identity to better understand the intersectional perspective of the candidate. Professional development becomes personalized and is void of stereotypes.

An executive at a major organization once said that he individualizes the experience for each of his clients in his residential homes. He has over 12,000 clients from all over the country, living in his residential homes at any one time. The managers at each of the residential facilities get to know their clients on an intimate level in order to understand how to serve them best. The leaders do not implement a "one size fits all" solution because they understand that their clients bring a lifetime of intersectional experiences, knowledge, and customs that shouldn't be discarded when they arrive. Organizational leaders should employ this same methodology with their employees.

Imagine an Intersectional Workplace

Intersectionality is not an attempt to throw out every diversity-related initiative and start over. However, leaders must do a better job of understanding how different identities work together to create a unique experience for someone. Intersectionality is about expanding the current definition of diversity and adopting a mindset of curiosity.

Imagine that you're a college-educated, African-American woman. You wake up every morning excited to go to work. You know that your boss is curious about the experiences you face and you can't wait to contribute your perspective to solve organizational issues. Your coworkers initiate and engage in conversations about your life in an attempt to understand where your unique ideas stem from. You are also curious. You want to learn about other people and how they experience the world because you understand how it enriches your life and your work. You share a picture of you smiling, with the caption #InMySkin, on social media because you know that you weren't always this comfortable at work. You wear your hair just as it grows out of your head, and aren't stigmatized because of it. You no longer feel the need to "code switch" or hang up your identity before you walk into your workplace. You speak using a vernacular most comfortable to you. You represent you, not an entire race or gender. You feel heard, appreciated, and valued. You feel safe. You are thankful that your organization embraces all of you, not just certain parts. You feel important.

By focusing on intersectionality, this can be reality for your employees.

Demetria Miles-McDonald

Demetria Miles-McDonald is the Founder and CEO of Decide Diversity, a company focused on increasing the presence and effectiveness of women and minorities in the workplace, specifically in leadership positions. Demetria's experiences in retail and corporate America have energized her to take action and lead a new generation of leaders away from traditional stereotypes and self-inflicted limiting behaviors that prevent qualified people from reaching their highest potential. Demetria specializes in bringing the experiences of people who identify with two or more marginalized groups to the forefront, to better understand the strengths they bring to the workplace.

Demetria has been in the business of helping people bring their best selves to work every day, for over 10 years in various leadership and organizational development positions. Demetria has a bachelor's degree in Psychology and a master's degree in Instructional Design. Demetria's unique perspective as an intersectional employee, leader, and researcher brings clarity, freshness, and focus to diversity issues at work that may otherwise go unnoticed.

Demetria experiences life with her supportive husband, Doren, and her loving dog, Dream. When she's not fighting for equality, Demetria enjoys spending time with her mom, dad, and sister.

To learn more about Demetria and her work, visit decidediversity.com or follow @*DecideDiversity* on Facebook and LinkedIn. For speaking engagements, training, and consulting, contact Demetria directly at **demetria@decidediversity.com**.

Jeff Nally

Four Steps to Spark Your Best Thinking:
A Brain-Based Approach to Being Human at Work

There's nothing more human about work than using your human brain at work. Employers say they want people to bring their skills and talents to work—but why is there so much mystery or even fear around actually *using* our brains at work?

Did you think using your brain at work meant acting like a know-it-all, calling yourself "wicked smart," or thinking of yourself as academically superior?

Good news: it's none of these. Thanks to neuroscience research, we know simple, effective approaches for everyone at work to interact in ways that are naturally friendly to our brains—and which can increase the brilliance of each person on every team.

Bring Your Best Thinking to Work

Employee engagement has, for more than a decade, been the standard to get employees to bring discretionary effort to work and to improve performance. It's the foundation behind many company mantras to "bring your whole self to work."

While this is an admirable approach to strengthen the connection between employees and their employer, it falls short of *being human at work*. It doesn't actually challenge people to bring their best thinking to work.

Far too often, employers only imagine their employees bringing their *current* skills, knowledge, and abilities to work. But as humans, we have so much more to contribute and to gain from working together.

What we really want is to have every leader, coworker, team member, and employee bring their best *thinking* to work.

The most profitable, favorable advantage for an organization is to have employees *who help each other think better at work*. The highest calling for a leader is to help her team tap into their uniquely human gift: their best thinking.

Don't We Already Think Enough at Work?

I have coached executives—and trained leaders to coach their teams—since 2006. I created the executive coaching practice at Humana, a health and well-being company, and coached hundreds of leaders in all areas of the organization for more than nine years.

Coaching engagements typically involved six months of coaching, with a coaching session every week or two. At the end of each coaching engagement, I asked my clients: "What was the most valuable aspect of the coaching experience?"

They always said things like:

"Our coaching sessions are the only times I get to think clearly."

"My work day is full of meetings and urgent problems to fix, so I never get time to reflect or think about the important things that can really make a difference for my team."

"This is the one hour each week I get to think about my thinking, when I can get insights into next steps that can really help me and the company."

That sparked my curiosity. I began to ask myself: "If coaching sessions are the only times that my clients get to do their best thinking, when do other employees do *their* best thinking?" I conducted a company-wide survey of employees to ask them: "When do you do your best thinking about the work-related problems you're trying to solve?"

The results shocked me: two-thirds of employees said they do their best thinking *outside* of work hours and *away* from the work team! In other words: two-thirds of our employees had valuable insights and solutions come to them when they were NOT at work—when they were outside of work hours, unable to take action, and unable to share them with co-workers!

So how many employees brought their best thinking *to* work? Only about one third.

At a time when the company was growing and healthcare (our industry) was facing new challenges, we needed everyone to bring their best thinking to the office every day.

Let me ask you: how successful can your organization be if only one-third of your employees do their best thinking at work? How successful could your organization become if *everyone* brought their best thinking to work?

What About Intelligence?

Let's clear something up: your *best thinking* is not the same thing as your *intelligence*. This is really not about who is more intelligent and who is less intelligent. There are plenty of systems already attempting to differentiate people in this way; employees don't want to spend eight hours a day working somewhere that makes them feel dumb.

My fifth-grade math teacher made it clear to everyone who the smart students were. Picture the students who went to the chalkboard and wrote the correct answer to math problems on their first try—or never made any mistakes on their math homework. The strong signal to the rest of us was: "**You** are not smart, **you** are not good at math, and I'm making sure everyone in the class knows it."

Our brains are always comparing and contrasting, letting us know where we stand in the pecking order of groups along criteria like intelligence and status, things that differentiate one person from the next.

There are times when this tendency can be helpful—like knowing who's in charge so we know whom to ask for help. But this tendency can also keep us from being more human at work. This tendency we all have can trigger feelings of inadequacy or inferiority, as my math teacher brought about in us.

Our brains put coworkers into categories, but in a manner primarily based on the emotions we experience—not based on any accurate assessment of how others can help us at work.

So how do we minimize the sense of negative status, categories, and emotions that diminish our best thinking?

Try these **four steps** to bring out each person's best thinking and help them be more human at work.

Step 1: Acknowledge that Each Person is Capable of Better Thinking

The first step to being more human at work: *acknowledge that each person is a whole, complete human being.* The people you work with may not be like you—but you can approach each day with the belief that those people are capable beings who can offer their own thinking, insights, and new ideas at work.

Nancy Kline, a coach and pioneer in the thinking movement, calls this the Positive Philosophical Choice. In her book *More Time to Think: The Power of Independent Thinking*, she describes this as a choice we make about the other person in our presence. When we make this choice, we are acknowledging to that person that "you are inherently intelligent, free to make real choices about your life and your feelings, able to think about anything, loving, creative, and worthy of good outcomes."

Leaders and managers often believe it's their duty to bridge the gaps in employees' thinking or intelligence or attention. This is a limiting belief, a drain on that leader's energy, and it stifles her own powerful thinking. Instead, seek out the sincere belief that each person is capable of clear thinking and meaningful contributions. Rely on humans at work to do what humans do best: *think!*

Step 2: Ask Questions That Generate the Best Thinking in Each Person

The second step is to be a leader or co-worker who asks questions that bring out the best thinking in others. This is what I do as a professional, credentialed coach: I ask questions that help clients think differently and gain clarity.

I am not suggesting that you should become a professional coach. Instead, I believe that anyone can learn to ask coaching questions to bring out the best thinking of the people around them. It's the greatest gift we can offer: the gift of a well-crafted question that ignites the best thinking in others.

What are well-crafted questions? They are questions *about the person's thinking* – not directly about the problem or challenge.

Well-crafted questions put the brain into a reflective mode which has a few effects. First, this reflection dampens negative or threatening emotions. Then it opens the executive functions of the brain (in the pre-frontal cortex) where insights and new thinking occur, and finally, it focuses us on current thinking and future possibilities.

Well-crafted thinking questions are often:

- Future-Focused Questions
- Scale Questions
- "Not" Questions

Future-Focused Questions

When people focus their thinking on the successful future, their brains enter a reflective mode – thinking about their thinking – instead of preoccupying itself with the current problem.

Some future-focused questions sound like this:

- What are you experiencing six months from now when this challenge is finally resolved?
- What do you see happening?
- What emotions are you experiencing? How do you feel?
- What are employees doing and saying?
- How do our customers feel? What are they experiencing?
- What are customers saying about our organization?

I led human resources in a company that experienced unprecedented growth by taking advantage of unexpected changes in the marketplace. I met with the senior executive team to create succession plans and determine development plans for the top talent across the company.

They acknowledged that they "got lucky" by hiring talented leaders away from competitors and paying millions of dollars in job search and placement fees to headhunters. They defined the current talent problem as unsustainable. They said, "If another unexpected growth opportunity comes along in the next five years, we won't be able to replicate the success we had in the past. How do we get leaders ready for the next big growth opportunity?"

I asked them, "Picture in your mind what's happening five years from now. A new growth opportunity came along, and we have all the leadership talent we need to succeed. What do you see?" They responded with:

"We have leaders with experiences that are different from our experiences. Leaders don't have the same demographics as our leadership team (mostly white males over 55 years old). Leaders define their own development pathways that give them broader business perspectives than we had five years ago. They don't have the same hang-ups, biases, or bad behavior that we demonstrate as an executive team." (Yes, they were very self-aware of their own challenges!)

Then I asked, "What's clear in your thinking right now?" and they responded with;

"We need to re-think our succession plans from 'who is next in line,' to 'what more does this leader need to learn to be ready for a variety of leadership roles?'

"Let's rethink leadership development from standardized programs to customized coaching experiences to accelerate individual learning and real-world practice.

"We need to rethink how we develop and grow leaders internally instead of paying for external talent that is likely to leave the company after two years on the job.

"Let's ask leaders what they want to lead five years from now, even if we don't have that role or business right now.

"Let's ask leaders to describe their best possible leadership situation five years from now, including the products and services they lead, the size of their team, the geographic location they want to lead from, and how they feel leading this type of business."

In this case, their best thinking generated a new approach to leadership development and succession planning. When new, unexpected growth opportunities came along a few years later, the company had multiple internal leaders who were capable and ready to lead several new businesses, products, and services.

Future-focused questions put the brain's emotions in a neutral to slightly positive state, silence our past experience, and spark new connections and ideas.

Scale Questions

Our brains think more clearly when we can measure our thinking. Yes, you can ask people to measure their own thinking! It sounds like this: "On a scale of one to ten, where 10 is 'crystal clear' and 1 is 'clear as mud,' how clear is your thinking about this issue right now?"

When the person responds with a number—for example, a six—ask them, "What makes your thinking a six instead of a one?" The person shares what's clear in her thinking, actions she may have already taken, or decisions she's already considered. This builds confidence in her ability to approach the problem. Her emotions are in a neutral to slightly positive state, activating her pre-frontal cortex and priming it for insights.

Then I ask: "What's the next thing you need to think about to make it a seven?"

When you ask the plus-one question, her brain begins to scan for insights and possibilities. She's using the executive functions of her brain – the parts of the brain we want people to use at work more often.

Her answer to the plus-one question is her next step. It may be a question she needs to answer, a topic she needs to think about, or an action she decided to take. It's the one thing that moves her forward, and that's a very different state than she was prior to your scale question.

I coached an executive using scale questions when he was unfulfilled in his current role and unclear about what to do. I asked him how clear his thinking was about what he wanted to do next; he said it was four out of ten.

I asked him what made it a four instead of a one, and he said that some of his previous jobs had been fulfilling and engaging, upward mobility in the current company was limited, and he didn't want to rebound to another company just to get away from his current situation.

I asked him what he needed to think about next to make it a five. He sat in silence for several seconds glancing to the right and left on occasion, and those were signals that his pre-frontal cortex was generating insights. I remained quiet while his brain did all the heavy thinking.

After a few seconds, he focused his attention on me and said, "I need to list all the things that I loved about my previous jobs, and that's what I need to look for in my next career move. I need to identify the criteria that I really want in my next job. That will make it a five." Now we're on to something!

For the next thirty minutes, he listed things he loved about the work environment and culture at a software company where he'd worked, the customer connections he'd enjoyed when launching retail department stores, the amount of travel he enjoyed (and the amount he hated), how meaningful relationships with coworkers made him feel, and his best leaders. These became the criteria he used to assess and pursue other career opportunities.

It wasn't long before he found exactly what he was looking for: an executive role with a start-up company that delivered products in a business-to-business model. It wasn't in the software or retail sectors, and he would never have found it without his new thinking.

The "Not" Question

There are times when our attention gets so focused on the problem that we're not thinking clearly or strategically. That's a good time to ask: "What have you *not* thought about that can be helpful right now?"

When we ask the "not" question, the brain starts looking for a missing puzzle piece, a story, a nugget of information, or something that might be useful. Our brains crave certainty and clarity, but most workplace problems aren't simple or easy to solve. If they were, computer programs could make those decisions. We need human brains – lots of them – to generate new thinking and solutions at work.

Asking the "not" question puts the brain into meta-search mode, seeking what we have not considered or thought about, and it won't rest until it gets some certainty and clarity.

I coached an executive who was hired to lead a team through reorganization. He was focused on the right things: keeping current employees engaged during the change, onboarding new employees, transitioning employees out of the team when necessary, redefining roles, and assigning new accountabilities. It was a time of tremendous change, yet he felt stuck. He wasn't sure what he should think about because all this attention was focused on the current changes.

I asked, "What have you *not* thought about that can help you right now?" He sat quiet for a long time, and so did I, careful not to interrupt his thinking or disturb the insight he was generating.

After a long pause, he said, "I haven't thought about what it will be like to lead this team when we get to a post-reorg, stable situation." Wow . . . sounds like a useful insight! He spent a few minutes describing what it would look like and feel like when the dust settled and the team was performing in its new state. He described it like a ship that had completed major upgrades and refurbishments, sailing to new ports with a new design and upgraded engines.

He saw his role as a strategic captain guiding the team's new direction. He saw the team as a skilled, knowledgeable crew who knew how to operate their respective departments. Now he was ready to craft action steps to become the captain of his new ship. It only took the "not" question to get his brain searching for new possibilities and to think through his next steps.

Step 3: Lead with Humility by Learning and Staying Curious

Whether you're a formal leader with a team or an informal leader collaborating with your coworkers, lead with humility.

I met with Dr. Brad Owens a few years ago to discuss his research, wherein leader humility led to greater team performance. I applied his findings to coaching and leadership development at Humana.

His research showed that leading with humility compensated for low intelligence, indicating that better thinking and solutions arise when people lead with humility, even when low intelligence doesn't seem to generate solutions. It also showed that teams experience greater performance when the leader has an appreciation of others' strengths and contributions and can remain open to new ideas and feedback.

Two behaviors—**curiosity** and **learning**—capture the essence of leading with humility.

Leaders who are *curious* seek out ideas from a variety of people and resources. The leader turns down his ego and turns up his sense of wonder, thinking outside himself to explore alternate solutions.

Learning leaders seek out new information, skills, knowledge, and insights to help them develop and grow. They have a learning orientation towards employees and acknowledge that leaders can learn from anyone in their organization.

Stay open, curious, and learn from others. Lead with humility. When there doesn't seem to be a simple or clear solution, ask,

- "What can I learn here?"
- "From whom can I get a different perspective?"
- "What kind of curiosity will help me see possibilities right now?"

Raise your brain power and be more human at work by leading with humility, staying curious, and approaching challenges with a learning orientation.

Step 4: Name Your Emotion, Tame Your Brain, and Gain New Thinking

We don't think without connecting to an emotion. Our thoughts and experiences are filtered through our emotions, even though we're not always aware of it. Acknowledging and naming emotions leads to new thoughts and insights. Here's how it works.

The limbic system is the emotional center of the brain. It colors and impacts our thoughts and experiences through emotions. The pre-frontal cortex's processing is compromised when our emotions are highly charged, as when we feel threatened. As we all know, emotions can interfere with our ability to take in information, think clearly, or draw sound conclusions.

Tame your brain by naming the emotion you experience. Accurately labeling the emotion—even a negative, defensive emotion—tames the limbic system.

This sounds counterintuitive. If I'm feeling furious and I say *I'm furious*, won't my brain just spiral deeper into more fury? No, it won't.

That's because our brain craves certainty and clarity. When I accurately name the way I feel, my brain experiences certainty and clarity. It's as if my brain says, "Sure, I know what fury is. I know what you mean when you say you're feeling furious. And now that I know what you're feeling, I can dampen that emotion so we can think."

The next time you're emotionally charged and triggered, simply name the emotion you're experiencing and you'll give your brain a chance to keep its balance and keep thinking.

What questions help you name your emotion, tame your brain, and gain new thinking?

- What's the emotion I <u>feel</u> when I think about this problem or situation? Name it and tame it.
- What's the emotion I <u>want</u> to feel when this is resolved? Name it and claim it.
- Is there a connection between my thoughts and my emotions that points me to a solution? If so, what comes to mind?
- What do I think about next—or do next—that gets me closer to a solution? Gain it and do it.

These questions are also useful to ask your team or coworkers. If we're facing a new challenge or trying to solve a problem, ask the team:

- What have you learned thus far? (*Remember that a learning orientation is part of leading with humility!*)
- What are the emotions that the team is experiencing? Name them so we can tame them.
- How does the team want to feel when this is fully resolved?
- What does the team want to think about next or do next that gets the team closer to a solution?

I was coaching the executive team of a company that had been acquired by a much larger corporation. They wanted to stay in the "command and control" mode, since that approach had helped them reduce costs and control every aspect of the customer experience. But now that they were part of a larger corporation, they were no longer the only ones in control of their business.

I asked the executive team the questions listed above, and here's what they said.

"We learned that we offer a specialized service that the acquiring company didn't offer and customers they didn't serve.

"We feel sad and angry that we're not in total control of our operations or our future.

"We feel pleasantly surprised at the number of people and resources the acquiring company offered to integrate our organizations. We feel grateful for the financial investment the acquiring company made in technology and hiring new talent.

"The connection we're making between our emotions and what we learned is that the acquiring company can help us reach more customers and improve our operations.

"The next thing we want to do is create a partnership with the acquiring company to implement the integration. We want to collaborate with the acquiring corporation."

There was still a lot of work to do and relationships to mend, but the executive team dampened their emotions and created new thoughts and actions about their future. They really wanted to grow, not command a declining business. They really wanted to connect with others, not control everyone in the process. They learned to be more human at work, even amid tremendous change.

Last but not least: *be human at work.*

- Bring everyone's best thinking into work; don't leave their best thinking outside of work.
- Acknowledge that each person is whole, complete, and capable of new thinking and ideas; don't rely solely on intelligence or assume someone is not intelligent.
- Ask well-crafted thinking questions of ourselves and the people around us to generate better solutions; don't seek just one person's answer or assume there is only one correct solution.
- Stay curious, learn from others, and lead with humility; don't lead out of pride or ego.
- Name emotions and get unstuck when our brains are negatively triggered; don't give in to impulsive reactions based on hijacked emotions.

Our greatest gift as humans is to use our brains—what makes us unique in this universe—to do meaningful work, and to connect to our fellow human beings so we bring out the best in one another.

ABOUT THE AUTHOR

Jeff Nally

SPHR, SHRM-SCP, PCC, RPCC

Jeff Nally is an executive coach, speaker, author, and coach supervisor who helps people to be more human at work. He is the president of Nally Group Inc., a practice that creates no-nonsense neuroscience applications to get results with the brain in mind.

Jeff has 25 years of professional experience in human resources, executive coaching, and leadership development in corporate and not- for- profit organizations. He leads workshops teaching leaders and teams to take the fear out of feedback, to coach for results using powerful questions, and to improve emotional effectiveness in the workplace.

He is a co-author of Rethinking Human Resources. Jeff was named one of the top Twenty People to Know in Human Resources by Business First of Louisville.

He is a certified Senior Professional in Human Resources (SPHR) from the Human Resources Certification Institute and a Senior Certified Professional from the Society for Human Resource Management (SHRM-SCP). He is a past chair of the Kentucky SHRM State Council and a past president of Louisville SHRM. He is the inaugural recipient of the Lyle Hanna Volunteer Spirit Award for his volunteer efforts to advance the HR profession.

Jeff is also a Professional Certified Coach (PCC) through the International Coach Federation, a Results Professional Certified Coach (RPCC) through Results Coaching Systems, and graduated with distinction with a Certificate in the Foundations of Neuroleadership from The Neuroleadership Institute.

Jeff holds a Bachelor of Arts in Psychology from Georgetown College and a Masters in Business Administration from Georgia State University.

EMAIL jeff@nallygroup.com
PHONE (502) 810-4116
WEBSITE www.NallyGroup.com
LINKEDIN /in/jeffnally
FACEBOOK /NallyGroup
TWITTER @jeffreynally

Gordon L. Peterson

Impact at Any Age:
How Boomers Can Thrive in the Millennial World

Much has been written since the Great Recession about the Baby Boomer generation (born between 1946 and 1965) working beyond traditional retirement age to rebuild their "nest eggs" after they were decimated during the financial collapse. So, too, as life expectancy increases, many Boomers are concerned about living beyond the time when their savings and investments run out, left to rely solely on Social Security (which is by no means a sure bet these days). Still other Boomers of retirement age remain on-the-job, not out of financial necessity but rather for the intellectual stimulation and social benefits that their work provides.

These factors have resulted in multiple generations working under the same roof, if not alongside each other (and there *is* a difference). Depending on the source rendered from a Google search, Millennials (people born between 1977 and 1995) make up between 40 to 50% of the workforce. Generation X (people born between 1965 and 1976) accounts for 25 to 30% of the workforce. Boomers make up the balance – roughly 25% of the workforce. Naturally, these figures can vary (sometimes significantly) by industry, but nonetheless, this dynamic further extends the definition of workforce diversity (a positive consequence). At the same time, this age diversity can heighten an organization's exposure to risks concerning unconscious bias and age discrimination.

Evolving Relationship Between Age and Contribution

It would be interesting to see the relationship between one's chronological age and the number of on-the-job work responsibilities handled by people at that particular age. Perhaps there is a researcher out there who has looked at this and not told me (I've tried looking). In general, I suspect there would be an inverse relationship: that as a person's age increases, they handle fewer responsibilities.

I'm not suggesting that, on one particular birthday when we arrive at work, our responsibilities suddenly plummet. But I do believe that over time, organizations tend to have a different set of expectations for different generations, and that the mix of quality and quantity somehow changes.

Are these changing expectations justified? Fair? Dangerous?

For example, do we somehow expect *less* from older generations? In my experience, I have been guilty of this prejudice and, I believe, also a victim of it (yes, I'm a Boomer, too).

I realize it's impossible to hold back the hands of time. I now proudly display my naturally grey hair after years of monthly trips to the salon for color. But for as long as I can remember, I have always been inspired by chronologically-older people who exude a youthful presence, one which has almost nothing to do with their physical appearance. I could never quite put my finger on what made them *youthful* but I was sure there was some common characteristic.

I am a Boomer who is determined to be seen as youthful by people younger than I am—a vibrant, relevant member of society—so I've been thinking more about those qualities. And as a Human Resources practitioner fighting the war for talent of any age, I believe there is an opportunity to increase overall organizational output and effectiveness by investing in the ongoing development of our Boomer workforce. How much is it costing us to *not* maximize the continued potential and productivity from all generations in the workplace, including Boomers?

You'll get no argument from me that Boomers can make great mentors and coaches for younger generations in the workforce – that we can hold invaluable institutional knowledge which is difficult to catalog or reference once we leave organizations. Serving as sages and whisperers can provide benefits inside many organizations, but the problem I have with these roles that Boomers may (arguably) be uniquely qualified for is that they sound so isolationist, non-inclusive, intangible, or soft.

Gather 'round, children—Grandpa is going to tell a story!

Is there not another way to look at the ongoing contributions from the Boomer generation—one that has not yet been more fully explored?

It's Personal

This topic really hits home for me. As I write this chapter, I'm two weeks away from my 57th birthday. I've had (what I consider) a rich and rewarding career so far. I am an unapologetically unconventional Human Resources professional who, at the age of 40, was asked to temporarily step out of an Account Management role to oversee the development and delivery of a sales training program within the same marketing firm. When that program was successfully completed, I had the opportunity to return to the Account Management role I had vacated—or, upon the invitation of the Chief Human Resources Officer, take a permanent position working for him in Learning & Development.

I chose to accept that invitation—and I never looked back! My responsibilities continued to grow over time such that, most recently, I was Chief Human Resources Officer for another large, global marketing and advertising firm.

In the summer of 2016, I embarked on yet another path within my career journey – one that I had not walked before. Effectively I was out of a job, due to a major restructuring of the organization. I was *not* caught off guard – the Officers of the company had been briefed months beforehand about the restructuring, and many of us knew that our jobs were in jeopardy. I explored a couple of different internal opportunities, but in the end, I ultimately decided to leave the firm.

Some of you may have experienced this situation at some point in your career, but this was new territory for me. I experienced a wide range of emotions, to say the least. I also experienced the stages of the change process through which I had coached so many others during my career. Only more recently have I been able to label the thing that I have been the most afraid of losing when I lost my job: my ability to make a value-adding impact.

Generating Impact is the Key

In today's knowledge economy, isn't impact the thing we ultimately get paid for? Isn't impact an accumulation of the effort, results, and contributions made? Financial value is placed on impact and gets translated into paychecks that get deposited into our bank accounts on a regular basis.

Identifying a handful of contemporary competencies Millennials are drawing upon to deliver impact in organizations today, and helping Boomers build proficiency in those competencies, will extend their organizational "shelf life" and garner greater returns for the entire organization.

Impact-Generating Competencies That Transcend Generations

Based on sustained, direct interaction and experience with hundreds of Millennials in my role as Chief Human Resources Officer, learning from firms who have their finger on the pulse of Millennials, and my own recent pulse-survey of 20-somethings, I would like to hone in on three "transgenerational competencies" that, when employed, produce value-adding impact. The three transgenerational competencies are **Future Focus, Learning Orientation**, and **Grit**.

These competencies are neither mutually exclusive nor collectively exhaustive, so the purist in me hesitates to label them *competencies* in the classic sense. Still, let's take a quick look at each of these... qualities, if nothing else. (I am not suggesting that Millennials have these competencies "nailed" naturally – they need to continually work on building proficiency in each of them, same as anyone else.)

Future Focus: It may seem obvious that Millennials have their eyes on the future because (God willing) they have so much life to look forward to. But the ability to anticipate, predict, and visualize future events or future states must be honed.

In my pulse survey administered to a sample of Millennials, I asked:

"Think about coworkers, managers, teachers, professors, friends' parents, your own parents or other family members whom you admire for their 'youthfulness', even though you know they happen to be over the age of 50:

- What qualities do they possess that impress you?
- What interests do they have?
- What do they specifically say or do that impresses or inspires you?"

Their responses were quite revealing, and instrumental in identifying all three of these competencies, but perhaps none more so than Future Focus. For starters, they indicated that people from older generations...

- "...don't reflect or dwell on the past..."
- "...they ask me really interesting questions and want to know my opinion about current events and what I think is going to happen in the future..."
- "...it's the opposite of 'burn-out' – it's like you can see their energy and enthusiasm for (what is yet to come)..."

Wow! What physicality there is in these responses! What possibilities and opportunities these responses create for individuals and organizations alike, right?

Learning Orientation: Millennials have fewer years behind them, matter-of-factly speaking, and they're likelier to have attended college recently. So Millennials have a hunger and thirst for *additional* knowledge. I am continually impressed that Millennials are always seemingly in pursuit of continuous self-improvement and are eager to experiment, to try new things out.

Again, from my Millennial pulse survey, there were some unanimous themes:

- "...they (people over the age of 50 with whom Millennials are impressed by their youthfulness) are continually learning and trying new things. They ask a lot of questions of the people they are around."
- "...you know, it's like they are the opposite of a 'know-it-all'". Because who likes a "know-it-all"?

Erika Andersen, in her book *Be Bad First: Get Good at Things FAST to Stay Ready for the Future*, argues that "learning well and quickly is the most important skill we can have." She goes on to say that "curiosity sends you to the new rather than away from it." It's interesting how this descriptor ties to our first competency, a focus on the future!

Grit: Look up "grit" and you will see that it is defined as tenacity and resilience. Koru, a leading firm in predictive, data-driven hiring and developing Millennial talent—includes grit among their seven "impact skills" they measure with their assessment tools. They define grit as the "ability to stick with it when things get hard. When directions are not explicit, hires (Millennials) can make sense of ambiguous situations."

I very much like Angela Duckworth's definition of grit. She is the author of *Grit - The Power of Passion and Perseverance*, and as the title suggests, she views grit as a combination of passion and perseverance. As a Boomer myself, these two levers really speak to me - I have lots of passion around what I do and what I'm interested in - and goodness knows I wouldn't have gotten to where I am today if I didn't persevere.

Getting Started

Thinking back on my childhood and the people one or two generations older than I who exhibited this age-defying youthfulness, I now realize that each of these people possessed these three qualities - a focus on the future, a devotion to lifelong learning, and grit. Now, as someone of a certain age who wants to be seen as vibrant, relevant (i.e. "youthful") by younger generations, I'm motivated by what I can do to build these muscles myself. And as a Human Capital consultant and professional development coach, I am intrigued by the incremental organizational productivity gap I can fill by helping Boomers increase proficiency in these three areas.

An entire book could be written on how to foster development in (and profit from) these things—perhaps a next step for me! For yourself, here are a couple of starting points.

1. I loathe New Year's Resolutions and haven't made (or kept) one in the usual form for years. But one commitment I did make to myself at the beginning of 2017 was to create and follow a personal learning "agenda" for the year. I have identified three things I want to learn more about this year and I've written a SMART objective for each of them. The topics I want to know more about will help me in both my professional and personal life. And I get "double- or triple-credit" because besides the obvious boost (Learning Orientation), one of my areas of learning is very much focused on the future. Lastly, to achieve this ambitious objective throughout the year, I'm going to have to show some grit!

2. Organizations and the people within them need to ask themselves: *how can Future Focus, Learning Orientation, and Grit help drive our long-term competitive advantage and revenue growth?* How can they help us execute well and achieve our business strategy?

Gordon L. Peterson

Gordon L. Peterson is a Senior Human Resources professional and independent consultant. Gordon has extensive business experience and has since migrated into Learning & Development and, finally, wing-to-wing Talent Management.

Before becoming an independent consultant, Gordon was Chief Human Resources Officer (CHRO) at Millward Brown, a part of the $70 billion WPP Group, for more than 5 years.

Gordon received a Bachelor of Arts in Communication Studies and began a career in market research as a consultant to the consumer packaged goods industry. He took on increasing levels of responsibility in Account Management roles before transitioning to Learning & Development and Talent Management.

Gordon is not a "traditional" HR professional (and unapologetically so!) given his extensive business/line management experience before moving into Human Resources. He specializes in Workforce/Pipeline Planning and Executive & Leadership Development. He also has extensive experience in Mergers & Acquisitions.

As a 50-something Baby Boomer, Gordon knows the sense that there's "runway" left in his career, but that others at work may not perceive it. His approach helps him remain vibrant, relevant, and energetic for contributing to the workplace of today and tomorrow.

You'll mostly find Gordon on the move; in his free time he's often working out, playing golf or tennis, traveling, or entertaining.

LINKEDIN /in/gordon-peterson-534217

Lisa Seay

Elements of the Lost and Found Spirit

Reflect back on your younger years when people asked what you wanted to be when you grew up. The possibilities were endless, weren't they? Recently, my daughter and her second-grade classmates were asked this same question as part of a class project. The boys and girls eagerly shouted answers ranging from teacher to dancer to even a puppet maker. The beautiful thing about youth and thinking about what's possible, is that it's ALL possible. And fortunately, no one tells you differently…until later. It's years later when parents start inputting what kind of degree they'll pay for, friends begin to judge your dream to backpack across Cambodia, and trusted adults tell you that you'll never make a decent living following your passion of pet sitter or dog walker. Maybe it's life circumstances that dictate you forego your planned education and attend the school of "hard knocks." Or possibly you're frozen in indecision, so put off clarifying your purpose and instead stay busy "doing life" until that just isn't enough anymore.

Perhaps my previous scenarios are not you. Instead, you are fortunate enough to have clarity regarding your dreams. You have people around you cheering you on and supporting you. You actually land the job that allows you to make the impact you imagined yourself making. You earn the necessary degree, are recruited by your ideal company, start your dream job, and begin your perfect adult life. The world is your oyster and maybe that's why – when down the road after you've been doing it for a while, "living the dream," – you abruptly hit a wall. Bit by bit that flawless vision of how you were going to contribute to the world through your profession and live out your calling doesn't seem right any more. Your calling starts to fade.

Or maybe you manage people who are coming to work spiritless. Their dissatisfaction becomes evident, yet because human behavior can be hard to discuss and alter, you ignore it, get angry, or worse, lash out and say something that you can't take back. But whether you're the leader of the spiritless tribe, or you are the spiritless one yourself, being able to recognize the signs and take action to reinvigorate that spirit is critical to long term success in your work, and more importantly, to long term happiness in your life.

How do I know this? Because I've spent years supporting people as a Human Resource leader, and in my experience, only rarely have I found myself solving problems with people who had so much energy and zest for their jobs that they couldn't contain themselves. They **in**frequently came to me to share great results of recent projects, or to discuss the fabulous work relationships they had built, or to revel in their delighted anticipation about the upcoming changes in the business.

Unfortunately, I heard mostly the opposite. It was typically hours upon hours of talking with those who were frustrated, discouraged, annoyed, angry, ignored, scared, timid, disrespected, uncertain, or unaware. Sometimes, they were even suffering from physical problems related to their work. The World Health Organization states that depression and anxiety lead to fifteen billion lost days of work a year, amounting to $1.5 trillion dollars lost annually. Many times, when an employee is experiencing a lack of connection to their core spirit, these feelings manifest themselves in toxic behaviors—which also have a price. According to a Harvard Business School report titled "Toxic Workers," workers in the top 1% in terms of productivity add about five thousand dollars to profit each year, while a toxic worker costs about twelve thousand dollars per year.

In addition to what I've witnessed through work, I understand career dissatisfaction personally. A couple of years ago, I hit that wall. I knew something needed to change. Everything wasn't wrong, but I just wasn't right. I wasn't bringing my best self to work, or home from work. Then one evening at dinner, when I began to lecture my five- and seven-year-old daughters about how they should behave when they got real jobs, I knew things were getting to me.

While having lunch with a friend who would later coach me through a monumental career change, I was asked the pivotal question: **what fuels your spirit?** After what felt like an eternity, I still had nothing. *What was so hard about this? This should be an easy question to answer.* Finally, I blurted out, "I don't know," and was hit with the realization that I might not ever figure it out.

Was it possible that what I'd been doing for the last twenty years had *killed* my spirit? And if so, how had I allowed this to happen? I had lost a sense of purpose about what I was doing. My spirit was being sucked out of me. Thus began the painful but necessary process of self-exploration. I realized this wasn't the way it had always been and was not how it was going to stay. It was important to recognize the signs of my depleted spirit and come up with a specific means of refilling the tank and, ultimately, restoring my purpose.

Why Does It Matter?

No matter the industry – whether providing services, products, or some combination of the two – the organization has no hope of achieving its ultimate potential without engaged and productive team members. That's why it matters. It matters if team members are walking around, contributing less than the best they have to offer, not realizing that their spirit—along with their drive, motivation and desire to do a good job—have vanished.

You know the ones – the employees you have to keep re-asking to do the job they should have been able to do the first time you asked. Another reason you should care is that your customers care—and they notice. They can tell when your employees are spiritlessly working. It shows in their sour demeanor while greeting or assisting customers. Or it's obvious by a less-than-stellar delivery on a project. It matters because disengaged workers cost, according to the Engagement Institute, between $450-$550 billion dollars a year. And that large a sum of money matters, especially to a business.

Elements of the Waning Spirit

What are some of the signs your spirit tank is running low? What about when someone on your team just doesn't seem to be engaged or contributing in the same way as others? Being able to mend a depleted spirit requires that you first see when it's waning. Here are four common scenarios that can hint that your spirit, or that of someone on your team, is running on empty:

1. Quick to Observe a Problem; Not so Quick to Identify a Solution

I love home improvement shows, especially the ones where the talented designers, who love what they do, transform a fixer-upper into a dream home; always to the amazement of a homeowner who saw only problems with the house until a vision of what could be was revealed. Somehow, I don't think these shows would have the same appeal if the designers didn't see possibilities. If they only saw problems, dead-ends, and obstacles, it's unlikely such programs would have much of an audience. This same ingenuity and passion signals a productive, happy worker. So, when you or an employee begins to spout a laundry list of why something can't be done, or, instead of seeing the opportunity a challenge presents, sees only obstacles and barriers, it's a sign that the tank may be approaching empty.

2. Much Ado About Nothing; Small Things Become Big Things

You've probably heard the phrase, "Don't sweat the small stuff... and it's all small stuff." One sure sign that a tank is starting to approach empty is too much focus on the minutiae. It's when you or a colleague start noticing that one person gets a compliment from the boss, but no one else. Or complain that your work station is a little smaller than the new hire's. Work becomes a series of tiny annoyances each day. Many times, these small grievances consume so much time – whether from stewing internally about them, complaining about them, or avoiding them – that they diminish performance.

3. Kindergarten or Work?

Surely this isn't you, but you may know someone who says things like, "He's not being nice to me," or, "She looked at me the wrong way." Maybe you're a manager and find yourself buddying up with the people who cause the fewest issues and excluding the others, who (in your opinion) are not as fun, pleasant, or interesting—in other words, choosing who to play with on the playground. There might even be a whiny tone in your voice. And when it's happening, you may or may not even notice – but I can guarantee you, others do. And unfortunately, they see a draining person they generally do not want to be around – let alone support, develop, or promote.

4. *What's the Point?* Not Convinced Work Makes a Difference for Employee, Customer, or Organization

Not knowing why you're there or if you make a difference is probably the most damaging thing to the spirit. Once an employee becomes disconnected from how they uniquely contribute to their work and how those contributions ultimately impact business for the better, it's hard to get anywhere.

A little after marrying my husband, I unknowingly found myself in the position to find true connection to my work. The job I had worked at didn't seem to be fully utilizing my skills or sparking my interests, and the company agreed, making me part of a reduction in force. Surprisingly, I'm now grateful for this experience because it helped me truly understand what it felt like to be laid off -- which I would later apply to help others through similar situations. This job loss also created space for what was to come. Shortly after starting a new job with a respected health care system managing their graduate nurse recruitment program, my husband was coincidentally diagnosed with lymphoma. Prior to my husband's diagnosis, I had no connection with work in a healthcare setting – which obviously and quickly changed. He was cared for by nurses who clearly had a connection to their purpose. They helped us deal with the unknowns of his disease, the side effects of treatment, the joy of the chemotherapy completion, and the anticipation of what was to come (and still is to come) in our lives. These nurses showed me what it looked like to *know* the difference your work is making for yourself, others, and the community. From that point forward, I was easily able to find a sense of purpose in recruiting future nurses. By hiring the best of nurses, I was assuring the next terrified young couple given unexpected news would have the best of care. That's how I would add value *and* help others to do the same.

Elements of The Found Spirit

Reconnecting with that lost spirit and refilling that tank is not impossible, but you do have to recognize that something's missing and be deliberate in your approach. Here are some tricks you can do for yourself, or for your team, that will help replenish what's missing:

1. Reconnect To What Makes You You

What's fuels your engine? What unique elements that when leveraged allow you to perform at your best? What are you doing when others see you making a positive difference? Often, the business of everyday life gets in the way of us connecting to what we do best or to our best qualities. While coaching people through periods of disconnection, my advice is to examine what is at their core and allows them to be their best. Then, treasure those special qualities and look for situations to share these natural traits, skills and abilities. Ultimately, it makes the ride so much smoother and more enjoyable.

2. Take Inventory of What's Missing

It's easy to identify what we don't like in our lives or what's not working for us. The harder challenge is to identify what you want *instead*. Identifying not only what you don't like, but what, if present, would bring greater meaning to your work, can bring *overall* greater meaning to your life. When people try to fix a broken car, but don't know what parts it needs to get driving, they find themselves spinning their wheels. They're staying busy, but not on the right things. It's like cooking, if I want to prepare a recipe, the ideal thing to do is identify the ingredients I have and the ones still needed. Once all necessary ingredients are obtained, I can create something delicious. Much the same in life.

3. Don't Waste Time Where You Don't Belong

Recently on vacation, I took my daughter horseback riding, guided by the most mannerly cowboy named Clint. He seemed to not only love what he was doing, but was exceptional at his job. Since we had nothing but time out on the prairie, I asked Clint what had lead him to his calling. He answered that by discovering what *didn't* suit him, he was actually able to confirm what *did* suit him and not waste any more time keeping himself from his passion. Our guide explained how he went to college, pursued the path he thought he was supposed to, and landed himself a dreaded desk job. Immediately he knew in his gut this wasn't a good fit; he actually told his new managers that they probably shouldn't waste any more time training him. Within two months, he packed up his stuff and returned to the country where he felt like his talents and gifts could be best utilized, and where he could be happy.

He ended our ride with a profound statement: "I guess it just depends on what you value." By knowing what *you* value, you can spend more time pursuing that and less wasted time spent on the things that don't contribute to what you value or to the value you want to create.

4. Broaden Your View of What's Possible

You're equipped. You alone know your strengths, what's missing from your work, and where you don't belong. So, it's time to explore – the fun yet often scary unknown. Exploration is where the gremlins show up. The fears and the what-if's. And, sometimes reality itself seems like a barrier. The reality of:

- I don't have the right education; or,
- I don't have spare time to look for another job; or maybe,
- I'm scared I won't be able to figure out what I'm good at; and then there's
- Things have changed so much in the job market, I probably should just stay where I am.

But what if your current reality – the one where your spirit is depleted – is really the thing to fear? When working with people on this topic, we first create an open space to imagine. Envisioning a new reality can be, in itself, the right tool to reignite your spirit. By imagining what's possible and building a plan toward it – that includes leveraging your strengths, identifying the missing pieces, and getting out of your own way – you can live a spirit-filled life at work that will surely translate to your personal life as well.

5. Saying Yes to Seconds

For me, instead of figuring out what I wanted to be when I grow up in second grade, I figured it out in the second phase of my career. Finally, I'd answered that once seemingly impossible question – what fuels my spirit? It's helping leaders and individuals contribute at their highest levels, and supporting them in building careers of purpose. By doing this, I make the work world a better place for all current workers and for those second graders who will be a part of it all too soon. And you can do it too.

Remember the advice of Dr. Seuss: "Today you are you, that is truer than true. There is no one alive who is youer than you."

Lisa Seay

MBA, SPHR, SHRM-CP

Lisa Seay is on a mission to help individuals find their professional purpose (and power!) and help companies develop cost-effective, efficient and sustainable talent management strategies.

As founder of the coaching/consulting firm **element c**, Lisa leverages her HR background to provide coaching, leadership development and team building services. By working in myriad environments during her 25-year corporate career—including Internet startups, mergers and acquisitions, franchised organizations, and large entities with multi-state locations—she knows firsthand how challenging organizational situations impact performance, employee engagement and personal career growth.

Before launching **element c** in 2015, Lisa held talent management and HR Director roles in a variety of organizations, including A.T. Kearney and Baylor Health Care System. Most recently, she served as a National Director of Human Resources at Conifer Health Solutions in Frisco, Texas, where she led a team that supported 3,000+ employees. During Lisa's tenure at Yum! Brands/Pizza Hut, Inc., she managed a $500K employee marketing initiative that attracted 250,000+ job seekers to the company's new online application system in three months.

A proponent of life-long learning, Lisa holds a Graduate Certificate in Executive Coaching from the University of Texas at Dallas and is a Certified Lumina Learning Practitioner. Lisa lives outside Dallas with her husband, Brian, who works in the financial services industry, and their young daughters. She is the New Family Liaison at Prince of Peace Christian School and also serves on the personnel committee at her church.

EMAIL lisa@theelementc.com
PHONE (214) 394-7308
WEBSITE www.theelementc.com
LINKEDIN /in/seaylisa

Rusty Steele

Strategic Volunteering:
Developing a Workforce of Compassionate Leaders

It's time to start thinking about employee volunteer programs strategically.

With the understanding that the long-term success of any company is directly tied to its human capital, companies are doing more than ever before to compete for and cultivate a good workplace.

The business world is constantly evolving, with a multitude of different programs and strategies that companies employ to positively position themselves to attract, develop, and retain the best employees.

If structured properly, a strategic employee volunteer program can help build a sustainable culture of compassionate leaders.

What I'm presenting to you is not the be-all end-all solution for developing leaders or creating a compassionate workplace culture, but merely a challenge to think about volunteering differently, and perhaps to add a creative tool to your toolbox that can assist you in your efforts to cultivate a compassionate culture.

A strategic volunteer program is more than just intertwined with an employee development plan; it is a program that engages its employees on an interpersonal level, guided by the compassionate belief that the company is as concerned with an employee's growth as a person as it is with their growth as a professional.

Transferrable Skills and Leadership Developed through Volunteering

The ethos of a compassionate workforce encourages all employees to think beyond their job duties to find ways to encourage, support, and empathize with one another.

Without compensation as a motivator, volunteer leaders must appeal to the most humanistic side of those whom they lead. To be successful, they have to be both purposeful and sincere, learning the strengths, struggles, and personal motivations of their volunteers. These leaders not only become skilled at compassionate leadership, but they desire to see others develop in the same manner, thereby creating a sustainable culture of compassion.

I've heard it said before that volunteering is a great laboratory for developing leaders, but I never realized the specific type of leader it developed until I was catching up with an old friend, whom I had met through volunteering. It did not take long to notice that something was different about her. The Jennifer I remembered was a quiet, reserved professional; however, now she seemed more confident and poised. She had always been a passionate volunteer, but she never wanted to be in charge, simply desiring to serve the community. As she continued to talk, it became clear that her passions and desire to serve were still there, but now they were focused not only on the community but also those who served around her, as well.

Jennifer embodies what it means to be a great leader. She is purposeful and personal in her actions and efforts, she leads her team of volunteers by appealing to their individual aspirations to direct, and supports them as they work towards a common vision. She believes the best way to serve the community is to serve those around her, mentoring and building them up in hopes of creating a culture of "servant leadership," as she called it.

In the few short years since I had last seen Jennifer, she had transformed from a passionate volunteer to a compassionate and effective leader.

Jennifer's story is great example of how volunteering can build compassionate leaders. It nurtures growth both as a person and professional.

Volunteering: The Practical Application Tool of Employee Development Programs

Employee development programs and volunteer leadership programs are both great tools for cultivating leaders, but in their most commonly employed format are both flawed. In order to understand how to intertwine these two programs, we must first understand those flaws.

The holes in employee development programs

Whether it is a business or nonprofit, any organization seeks leaders to support its growth, mission, and long-term goals.

To prepare for future growth and maintain organizational knowledge, businesses have implemented employee development programs and tools focused around a variety of leadership skills. These programs can include training in communication, engaging and motivating others, time management, delegation, planning and organizational skills, team management, project management, and more. These programs are great tools to increase an employee's knowledge, but too often they are classroom-based and provide little to no opportunities for employees to apply the knowledge and/or leadership skills that they learned.

Leadership is like driving: it takes time, practice, and patience to get good at it. Putting an employee who has conceptual knowledge of leadership but very little practical application into a leadership position is the equivalent of putting your son or daughter through a driver's education class—and then, without any other driving experience, giving them their license and keys to your brand new car. It can be a risky and frightening situation.

An employee is given the conceptual knowledge to be a successful leader, but that knowledge needs to be applied, practiced, and reinforced for it to truly set the employee up for success.

The fewer opportunities the employer has to observe an employee's leadership in action, the more difficult it can be to assess if an employee has the ability to lead to the level required by that position. This is a challenge which many employers face. It's not that they don't desire to provide the employee with opportunities to hone their leadership skills; it's just difficult to manufacture leadership opportunities for an employee whose current role and/or compensation doesn't already account for a leadership position. This can sometimes lead to an employee who is unprepared being promoted, or the company deciding to hire an external candidate who has the necessary proven leadership experience.

The holes in employee volunteer programs

Employee volunteer programs have been around for quite some time, and though they have become commonplace, they haven't evolved all that much. Employers who are good corporate citizens are offering more incentives for employees to volunteer, but few are actively engaging with employees' volunteer interests.

Employee volunteer programs ,are being utilized more frequently as more and more companies are recognizing the value they can bring to their company. There are a number of reasons companies support these programs, whether it is a desire to be a good corporate citizen, brand marketing, networking/sales opportunities, recruitment, retention, or others.

In spite of their increased prevalence, there are still too few employers who recognize employee volunteer programs as a vehicle for leadership development, and even fewer still who approach and structure them in a strategic manner to capitalize on the growth and development offered through employee volunteerism. The other major issue is that while most employers support employees' involvement in volunteer programs, some don't know why employees become involved in the first place. While some companies communicate about this topic, they can sometimes be more focused on the "what" instead of the "why." If you want to build a workforce of compassionate leaders, then you must first learn their passions and intrinsic motivators for their involvement, actively engaging with an employee's volunteer interests.

Unhappy ending

To drive this point home, I'd like to share the second half of Jennifer's story. I just told you how her volunteer involvement had grown and developed her as a person and professional, visible in both her accomplishments within her volunteer organization and the subsequent effect it had on the way she carried herself.

As powerful as the beginning of this story was, there is an unfortunate ending, given how these accomplishments and improved leadership were viewed by her employer.

A leadership position had opened up at Jennifer's company. She was the most qualified internal candidate; she had the tenure, organizational knowledge, and leadership experience required to be successful if promoted.

This position would require a much higher level of leadership than her current role. Jennifer knew this would be the committee's biggest concern in considering her for this position. She was confident nevertheless, feeling she had not only taken every leadership opportunity provided within her current role, but had also personally invested into her own growth as a leader within her volunteer organization and her community.

In the interview, she discussed the leadership skills she had developed and refined through her volunteer experience, what she had accomplished within her leadership roles, and how that could translate to her success in the role for which she was being considered.

Jennifer was then regrettably informed that they couldn't consider her volunteer work as leadership experience because it was with a "trade organization."

This is a perfect example of a company that could benefit from implementing a strategic employee volunteer program. The issue wasn't that they didn't appreciate her volunteer leadership or accomplishments; in fact, their company encourages employees to volunteer. The issue was that they hadn't engaged with her on the front end of her volunteering journey. Without doing so, they had no frame of reference to evaluate those leadership positions and accomplishments, or how transferable they were.

Strategic Volunteering Program Design

At this point we've established the value that can be realized from strategically aligning your employee development programs with your employee volunteer programs in order to create a culture and employee base of experienced, loyal, and compassionate leaders. What I'd like to discuss next is what this looks like in application.

One stone at a time

It is important to remember that you can't accomplish everything all at once. Start on the path of least resistance and build piece by piece. You will want to approach designing an employee volunteer program like you're trying to drain a river by removing stones. The stones are obstacles that you will have to overcome. As each stone is removed, the water level will lower, and as the water level lowers, more stones will be revealed. Start with the stones you can see. Even if you know what stones are lying under the surface, don't put yourself under water to remove them; they will be much easier to remove once the water level is lowered. This will allow you and your company to build the program in a sustainable manner.

I am about to discuss a series of ideas and areas for building this program. These are concepts to help aid idea generation for the overall vision of your program, but in no way is this list comprehensive or in a strategic order. You will need to tailor it to your company, taking into account where your company is currently at on this journey, and any unique obstacles it may face.

Hire people that will help you drain the river

We will start with the first moment that the employee interacts with your company professionally. Every company has their own unique interviewing strategy and selection criteria. Regardless of whether your company's interviews are structured or unstructured, every company strives to make the right hires, focusing not only on the knowledge, skills, abilities, and experience needed for a candidate to be successful, but also evaluating if a candidate's core values are congruent with your company culture.

Regardless of the experience the candidate has, hiring a candidate whose core values don't align with your desired or established company culture is like adding stones to your river: it will raise the water level. I would encourage you to review your company's hiring and selection criteria to assess the weight that is put on volunteer involvement. Ask yourself if you look at a volunteer position as a previous/current job. Would you be asking similar types of questions for a volunteer position? Do you try to understand why they volunteered? Do you assess their personal growth and development? Did they have a leadership position? Whether you're trying to build a culture of compassionate employees or trying to maintain one, hiring employees who fit this culture is key. Culture is precious and fragile; you want to be sure you're adding people who will help you identify and remove stones.

Make a casserole out of your employees' personal and work selves

In order for a company to build great leaders, it must first engage those employees on the most humanistic level possible.

As Jim Collins says in the book *Good to Great,* "the X-Factor of great leadership is not personality, it's humanity." In order for a company to build a sustainable culture that creates compassionate leaders, it needs to do more than educate and train employees; it must blur the lines between the employee's personal, philanthropic, and professional goals.

These leaders take a personal stake in their employees; they know what they care about, what they are passionate about, and what their dreams are.

This is one of the most critical and likely most challenging steps of this process. The following are a few tips and tools that should help guide you in this process.

As Simon Sinek says in his acclaimed TED Talk, you have to start with the why. You need to engage the employee on a very personal level in order to ascertain why the employee chose to volunteer at a specific nonprofit, what about this cause speaks to them as a person, and what they found rewarding about their involvement. Have a conversation to learn about it. Each employee will have different motivators; some volunteer for professional growth and some volunteer to give back to the community, but most commonly you will find it is a little of both.

It is important to approach this conversation with the understanding that most employees are used to the generally-accepted business culture that views an employee's work self and personal self as separate dinner courses; we all accept that they are on the same plate, but try to keep them from touching as much as possible.

Because of this, some employees may be hesitant to talk, so plan accordingly.

Be open about your goals for the conversation. They have to know the employer's "why" in order for them to feel comfortable sharing theirs. If they understand that your goal is learn more about each employee's volunteer involvement in order to see how the company can help support them, they will be much more likely to open up about their personal philanthropic passions.

Some employees will already have a list of philanthropic goals identified; however, some will need assistance. Identify their vision. This is the easy part. Ask open ended questions about their volunteer organization's struggles and growth opportunities, as well as things it could do to further its mission.

Some of these visions will be grander than others. Don't try to fit their dreams into a box. Meet the employee where they're at. You don't want to discourage big thinking. Regardless of the magnitude, it is critical to help them determine what their milestones are.

Integrating volunteering into employee development training

Armed with this information and having established an open forum, you have everything you need to integrate an employee volunteer program into this process. Determine what areas they will need to develop personally or professionally in order to achieve their dream, and then incorporate those into the training that you provide them in their employee development program. Due to the fact that nearly all skills needed to lead in a volunteer organization are transferable to the skills needed for leadership in the workplace, this shouldn't require a complete overhaul of your employee development programs.

Employees will be more engaged with their training knowing that they have volunteer platforms to immediately implement, practicing and refining what they are learning in the workplace. This will maximize employees' development and knowledge retention.

Performance reviews and follow-up

One of the keys to making this a sustainable program is proper follow-up.

Though this should be an ongoing conversation, it is important to establish follow-up procedures to determine how employees are progressing, encourage and coach them through setbacks, celebrate their successes, evaluate what they are learning, and determine if new goals need to be set.

Aside from following up at touch points and progress checkpoints, I encourage you add more follow-up to the employee performance review process; not that you as an employer are evaluating or judging an employee's performance as a volunteer, but more so to reinforce that you as an employer sincerely care about your employee's personal aspirations, and view these aspirations as just as important to their professional development. This will also provide an opportunity for the employee to offer feedback on the program and any ideas they may have to improve it.

Be prepared to mentor and coach your employees as they start to face the challenges that come along with leadership. This will give you invaluable information when it comes time to determine whether or not an employee is ready for a leadership role within your company.

Invite the Employee to Bring Their Whole Self to Work

We've discussed the benefits that your company can reap from having an employee volunteer program that is strategically designed to complement and fuel employee development, but we haven't discussed the positive effects it can have on your organization's culture.

Early in my career one of my colleagues said, "The only reason that employees complain is because someone listens." Though this statement was said in jest, it unfortunately typifies how some leaders view empathy as it relates to leadership. They fear that showing too much kindness can be viewed as a sign of weakness.

In reality, the opposite couldn't be more true. The benefits of a compassionate workplace are well known and supported by research.

What does a compassionate workplace look like?

A compassionate workplace is one in which employees are actively and sincerely engaged in supporting one another personally and professionally. It is an environment that focuses on driving collaboration and learning through inclusiveness and empathy. These employees have a greater appreciation for the value that each person's role contributes towards the company's success, with an understanding that for the company to be successful they have to continue to support each other.

Encourages employees to bring their personal passions, desires, and struggles to work

Strategic volunteering programs are great for reinforcing compassion in the workplace.

Invite humanity into your workplace. When an employer takes the initiative to engage employees on an interpersonal level, with a sincere desire to nurture and support their personal goals, it creates a safe place for employees to bring more of themselves to work, nurturing a more compassionate self.

Encourages employees to reciprocate the compassion modeled by management

Compassion is contagious. When management is actively working to support employees, it elicits a desire to reciprocate.

Employees will want to engage their peers in the same manner modeled by management, by first engaging on an interpersonal level, then actively looking for ways to support them As employees receive support, whether it be emotional, professional, or philanthropic, it causes them to look for ways to pay it forward. This helps build stronger bonds and is the foundation for compassionate leadership.

Showing compassion doesn't just help that peer. It supports community.

A strategic volunteer program aligns the success of the business with the success of the community through supporting its employees' volunteer efforts. With this in mind, employees are not only more likely to volunteer for their own personal growth, but also will be more willing to support and be involved in their peers' volunteer efforts, with the understanding that doing so supports more than the individual but also the company and community.

Summary

A company that attracts, retains, and engages employees who are invested in the big picture and understand the interconnectivity of their volunteering efforts and the community's goals will reap the benefits of a loyal and engaged employee base that has the ability not only to lead compassionately, but to lead with the end goal in mind. These passionate employees are forward-thinking, not only seeing the direct correlation between achieving organizational success and their success and growth as a professional, but also understanding that as the company grows, so does its ability to support the community to which it belongs and the causes it cares about.

Adding a little strategy to your employee volunteer programs can add a lot of compassion to your culture. This will take time, effort, and patience—but as my friend Jennifer might say, you might feel you get just as much out of it as the people you help.

ABOUT THE AUTHOR
Rusty Steele
SHRM-CP, PHR

Rusty Steele is Human Resource Manager for Neill-LaVeille Supply Co. in Louisville, Kentucky. His work experience includes both Human Resources and Operations Management, which gives him a unique perspective for evaluating business decisions and taking into account both HR-related outcomes and a business's bottom line.

Rusty began his career with a staffing and recruiting firm and was promoted within six months to HR Manager for Worldwide Technologies and its two sister companies. Two years later, he was promoted again to Operations Manager for one of those sister companies. For the next three years, he filled dual roles as Operations Manager and HR Manager for three different entities.

Rusty has a passion for volunteering. He discovered this passion during his undergrad at Western Kentucky University, with groups like Delta Tau Delta and Student SHRM no less (which he and his classmates helped re-establish there). For the past eight years Rusty has volunteered in various roles and capacities for SHRM.

Rusty dedicates this chapter to his mother Kimberley Flake. Thank you for raising us to fervently pursue even our most impossible dreams. Now it is our turn to help you chase yours—your story is just beginning.

EMAIL rusty.steele07@gmail.com
PHONE (270) 303-5351
LINKEDIN /in/rusty-steele-shrm-cp-phr-2068b43b
TWITTER @Steele_HR

Tracy Stuckrath

Food and Beverage at Work:
Workplace Solutions for Employee Well-Being and Inclusion

Food is everywhere. When two people get married, we celebrate with a banquet. When someone is born or dies, we bring food. Promotions, birthdays, retirements, you name it... food is served. So are beverages. And food has become the focus of every social outing.

The food environment at work is no different. Food is the common denominator of company picnics, holiday celebrations and staff meetings. There are employee refrigerators, staff kitchens, vending machines and corporate cafeterias, and food is provided at sales conferences and incentive trips. What isn't consistent, however, is the type of food served. This chapter discusses how companies can improve employee well-being by serving healthy, safe, inclusive meals—and why they should.

* * * * *

In recent years, the dramatic rise in corporate health and wellness programs shows that companies understand (or are beginning to understand) the benefits of a healthy workforce. According to the Society for Human Resource Management, more than two-thirds of U.S. employers currently offer a wellness program as part of their benefits packages.

The main focus is on exercise and a healthier diet, but unless these programs address everything employees are eating, they are doomed to fail. Take, for example, the case study presented by Alison Acerra, MS, RD, a national nutrition and wellness manager for Guckenheimer, a national workplace foodservice provider. The case was presented during an episode of the *Workforce Health Engagement* podcast, hosted by Jesse Lahey, SPHR.

Guckenheimer's client had recognized that it had a significant problem with increasing health care costs, rising insurance rates, and decreasing productivity. After issuing company-wide biometric screenings, it confirmed that 29 percent of its workforce had Metabolic Syndrome (caused primarily by insufficient exercise and a diet rich in sugar, salt, and fat). Senior executives quickly engaged experts to help them evaluate employee health and develop a wellness program with incentives, in hopes of seeing major improvements.

Unfortunately, the results were very disheartening. While reassessing the wellness program, the company realized why it wasn't working: the food and beverage offerings sold to employees in the company cafeteria and vending machines were more likely to promote disease than prevent it.

After revamping the on-site cafeteria to make it more health-focused, and nudging employees to choose healthier options with strategic positioning and pricing subsidies, Metabolic Syndrome rates dropped 11 percent in three years. The company also saw a $1.5 million reduction in health care spending.

The results of the Guckenheimer program are not unique. Research indicates that when companies genuinely support and promote the well-being of their workers, the rewards go beyond just health-related cost savings. Building a culture of wellness and fostering holistic employee well-being helps create a healthier, more engaged and loyal workforce— employees who deliver a difference both for their teams and their departments.

A recent study conducted by the Economist Intelligence Unit and sponsored by Humana found that, across all areas of employee health and well-being, there's a significant difference between those workplaces that have created a culture of wellness and those that have not.

A 2015 Health and Well-Being Study conducted by the O.C. Tanner Institute found that improved well-being has a large impact on employees, the way they work, and ultimately on the company's bottom line. It found that, as employee well-being increases, the positive effects resonate throughout the organization, and teams become more productive, more collaborative, and more prepared to innovate.

Wellness and well-being are not the same. Wellness programs have traditionally focused on exercise, meal plans and healthier snacks. However, well-being is much more. It evaluates a person's perception of the quality of his or her life. Is my life fulfilling and satisfying? Does my employer respect and appreciate me as a person? How do I feel today? The O.C. Tanner report says that understanding employee well-being as a holistic life experience shows a much more extensive definition of the term.

The study's results found that an employee's well-being is largely affected by three dimensions of wellness—physical, emotional/mental, and social:

- Physical wellness includes both positive health habits, such as seeing a doctor and losing weight, and negative health habits such as smoking.
- Social wellness is grounded in work-life balance and the presence of quality interactions with others both at work and at home.
- Emotional wellness takes into consideration how well talents are utilized at work, feelings of belonging, stress levels, liking work beyond just a paycheck, having purpose in your life, and feeling a sense of control.

As we will see, providing healthful food goes a long way toward fostering well-being in the workplace—but it's not enough.

* * * * *

Today, more than ever, there is a growing occurrence of individuals with special dietary needs. Some have medical conditions such as food allergies, diabetes, and gluten sensitivity. Others have made a health-related or moral commitment to eating vegetarian, pescetarian, vegan, organic, or paleo. Still others observe religious diets like kosher and halal.

Let's take a look at some current statistics on the number of people with dietary needs.

- 15 million Americans (5 percent of the U.S.) have food allergies, nine million of whom are adults.
- Diabetes is the epidemic of the 21st century — the number of people with diabetes has risen from 108 million in 1980 to 422 million in 2014. More than 29 million Americans (9.3 percent) have diabetes and another 8.1 million (27.8 percent) have undiagnosed diabetes.
- One in every 133 people has celiac disease (1 percent of the U.S. population). Ninety percent of them have not been diagnosed yet. And 18 million people have non-celiac gluten sensitivity.
- Close to 16 million people (5 percent) of the U.S. population are vegetarian and about half of these vegetarians are vegan.
- More than two-thirds (68.8 percent) of U.S. adults are considered to be overweight or obese. More than one-third (35.7 percent) are considered to be obese.
- As of 2012, almost 50 percent of all U.S. adults—117 million people—had one or more chronic health conditions. One of four adults had two or more. Chronic diseases include heart disease, stroke, cancer, type 2 diabetes, obesity, and arthritis.
- A 2010 CNN poll showed that 36 percent of the population follows a religious-based diet, almost on a daily basis.
- According to *Kosher Nation: Why More and More of America's Food Answers to a Higher Authority*, only 14 percent of the 11.2 million Americans who regularly buy kosher food are observant Jews. The rest are Muslims, Seventh-Day Adventists, vegetarians, people with food allergies and other consumers who feel safer following the strict rules of kashrut than standard USDA guidelines.

Employees who maintain special diets for medical, health and/or religious reasons are often faced with a limited selection of food options at work. Some must avoid foods that might cause an allergic reaction, or refrain from eating animal products, foods high in fat, salt or cholesterol. For others, their culture and religion dictate when and what they eat.

Recognizing and appreciating these needs can help employers provide food and beverages that are not just healthy but also safe and inclusive attributes critical for well-being.

Take Alex, for example. She is a state government employee with a severe life-threatening allergy to shellfish. Her allergy is so severe that she cannot be in the same room with it.

Two weeks into her job 10 years ago, she informed her boss of her allergy when a coworker sitting next to her had brought shellfish for lunch. Her boss informed the woman of Alex's allergy and asked her not to eat seafood at her desk or on the floor.

Each time the woman or others on her floor would bring seafood to eat at work, Alex would ask the Human Resources department to do something about it. The head of HR would simply ask them to stop bringing in the offending food, but refused to put a sign up.

After losing two weeks of sick leave within a three-month time frame because she was rushed to the hospital with allergic reactions that occurred in her office, Alex visited the Massachusetts Commission Against Discrimination to get her employer to comply and provide notification about her allergy in the workplace. It took the company three and half years to put up signs on her floor. After a few years, the signs were taken down.

While she is grateful to have information in her workplace about her food allergy, she feels her employer only provided it to avoid a lawsuit. Managers have not created an environment where her needs and her health are respected or appreciated. And, while Alex's productivity has not been affected—except when she was in the hospital recovering—her loyalty and morale towards and within the workplace have waned. She is looking for another job.

* * * * *

Any good Human Resources professional understands that fostering a safe and inclusive workplace is good business—but in some cases, it is also the law. While special dietary needs are not new to society, the practical and legal issues surrounding the accommodation of dietary restrictions at work, in school and elsewhere, are changing and affecting corporate bottom-lines.

One reason that there is not more awareness around dietary needs in the workplace may be the perception among Human Resource professionals, legal departments and corporate executives that the risk of liability for food allergies and other dietary needs is slight.

Attorney Tyra Hilliard states in a piece for Hotel Business Review that: "While the Rehabilitation Act of 1973 and the Americans with Disabilities Act of 1990 (ADA) were anti-discrimination laws intended to require accommodation for persons with disabilities, they were construed quite narrowly by the courts. Resulting case law citing these Acts was not favorable to persons with food allergies."

The Rehabilitation Act applies to programs and organizations who receive federal funding. The ADA was passed as an effort to expand the anti-discrimination protection of persons with disabilities to those in the private sector. As Hilliard points out, these laws were traditionally not interpreted to consider dietary restrictions as a disability. Not until 2008, that is.

In that year, in response to case law that narrowed protection and made inclusivity in the ADA an uphill battle, the ADA was amended (to the ADAAA) to better fit the spirit of the law as it was originally intended. The amended law broadened the definition of "disability" by modifying key terms that define it. The list of "major life activities" was expanded to include, but not be limited to seeing, hearing, eating, walking, standing, speaking, breathing, and working as well as "major bodily functions," which includes the immune, digestive, bowel, neurological, brain, respiratory, circulatory and endocrine functions. Notice that "eating," "immune" and "digestive" functions are all included in the amended law.

The changes to the ADA have had a powerful impact on organizations. There is a greater risk of negligence liability regarding food allergies and other dietary needs in the workplace. Discrimination based on dietary needs can take the form of harassment, bullying, threats, retaliation by coworkers and companies themselves, not to mention ignoring employee needs when providing food and beverage in corporate cafeterias and vending machines, and at company meetings and events.

Take, as an example, the 2015 lawsuit filed by Dustin Maldonado, a 26-year-old man with multiple food allergies, including peanuts and tree nuts, against his former employer, Panera, LLC, for severe and pervasive discrimination based on disability. The complaint outlines conduct by Dustin's general manager and coworkers that included a "campaign of humiliation led by management, threats that the disabled employee would be poisoned, and retaliation when the employee sought protection from Panera headquarters."

On multiple occasions, Dustin was not only taunted about his allergy by his general manager and other employees, but he was also tricked into eating foods that contained tree nuts. There were threats that his coffee would be poisoned, and he was teased that his EpiPen would spread AIDS. When he sought help from Panera headquarters in stopping the dangerous and discriminatory behavior, the HR department told Dustin, who has had to be intubated after exposure to peanuts in the past, that he should have more of a sense of humor.

Although we don't know how much Panera ultimately paid out—the lawsuit was settled out of court—the situation brings to the light the financial and legal implications that can result from not creating a workplace where all employees feel welcome and treated with dignity and respect.

Note that religious dietary needs are also protected under law. Title VII of the Civil Rights Act of 1964 prohibits religious discrimination in the workplace and requires employers to reasonably accommodate an employee when that employee's sincerely held religious beliefs, practices, or observance conflict with a work requirement, unless the accommodation would cause an undue hardship to the employer.

Accommodating religious based scenarios, including religious diets, have garnered a great deal of attention in recent years, and religious discrimination claims filed with the Equal Employment Opportunity Commission have almost doubled since 2000.

* * * * *

Not all food disabilities are life-threatening, the way Alex's and Dustin's are. When the consequences of eating a restricted food aren't immediately obvious, others — at work, school or even at home — sometimes doubt the illness exists, and accuse sufferers of simply angling for special treatment.

Wendy has celiac disease, an illness in which gluten—found in wheat, rye and barley— triggers an autoimmune response that destroys the lining of the small intestine. She has worked at three different companies after being diagnosed. Her experiences at each company show that creating a safe and inclusive environment is important.

At a real estate company she worked for, there were weekly, mandatory lunch meetings catered by Olive Garden. After some pressure, a gluten-free meal was provided, but then she was informed that it would not be done again. The next time they allowed people to bring their own food.

At a municipal public service job, the mandatory lunch meetings always had food provided for employees with special dietary needs, with no argument or problem. Gluten-free snacks were also available and set aside so she and two other coworkers with celiac disease could enjoy. "There was never any question that we would be taken care of," she said. "It made me feel valued and appreciated as an employee that my needs were being met and that I could participate equally with my coworkers. Cleaning the break area was part of the housekeeping staff's duties, and I felt safe eating in the break room."

At her current job, there is an annual all-day training session with lunch included. She has spoken to the organizers every year about having gluten-free food available, but she is always told to bring her own food since no special arrangements will be made for her or anyone else. This behavior or unwritten policy makes her feel as though she is an inconvenience to the organizers and not as important as the rest of the staff. She says: "Allowances are always made for mobility or impairment disabilities, but not celiac disease. While I know that the law simply states reasonable accommodation is required, and that includes allowing me to bring my own food, the social aspect of sharing a meal with people is somewhat lost, and I could be labeled as a 'picky eater' since I am not able to participate in the provided meal."

* * * * *

People with life-threatening allergies are generally vocal about their needs, but people like Wendy, whose dietary restrictions are not a life-and-death situation, and people with religious restrictions, may conform to social pressure. Consider this case study:

A meeting planner manages and hosts recruiting events for employers. The weeklong events bring in thousands of young applicants to meet with potential employers of Fortune 500 companies. Since she has food allergies herself, she works diligently with the hotel staff to ensure that everyone can eat safely.

Last year, at the final dinner where the applicants were dining with the employers most likely to hire them, the hotel told the planner that her special meal requests were way off… none of the special meals had been requested. She could not figure out why, since all week they were spot on.

She discovered that the applicants did not request their "special" meals because they did not want to be looked upon as burdensome employees who might cause hassles in the workplace. This phenomenon, called "covering," coined in 1963 by sociologist Erving Goffman, also occurs when young women remove their wedding rings to prevent potential employers from assuming that they will leave work to have children.

Covering is unacceptable on many fronts. But as Kenji Yoshino and Christie Smith point out in their study, Uncovering Talent: A New Model of Inclusion, most inclusion efforts do not address the pressure to conform to workplace standards. For example, an Indian man accepted the chicken salad plate presented to him at lunch, and ate only the lettuce around the chicken, because he did not want to ask for a vegetarian meal. John, a vegan who was interning at a company who offered him a job upon graduation, was not partaking in the intern pizza lunch. Instead of asking if a vegan pizza could be ordered, he ate the iceberg lettuce instead. And Beth, a vice president of talent management and diversity, is a vegetarian diabetic. She has the power to ensure that special meals are brought in, but when lunch is ordered, instead of rocking the boat, she subsists on pickles and potato chips.

When hosting events for current and potential clients, do you inquire about their dietary needs? Ignoring the needs of your client could make or break a sale. David learned this when he was preparing for a lunch presentation and had a couple of new consultants at his client's firm. He had started a practice of sending standard, gluten-free and vegan menus to his clients "to let people figure out what they would like to eat instead of getting stuck with another round of pizza or sandwiches." He had heard one of the new guys was hard to get along with. Little did David know, that by sending over different menus, he was able to meet the new person's dietary needs, so that consultant didn't have to sit through the presentation watching everyone enjoy their lunches while he was "eating his second piece of lettuce." Giving everyone a meal choice began the relationship on a positive note. David and the consultant have since worked together on other projects.

* * * * *

So how can a company create an inclusive and safe food and beverage culture that supports employee well-being for each person? For starters, Tess O'Brien, an attorney at Boardman & Clark, LLP, who provides legal consultation to educational institutions on disability law, says employers are not doing themselves any good ignoring employees with food allergies or other dietary needs. You do not want anyone to die, nor do you want to discriminate against them. She says employers should be proactive, have plans in place and provide training.

It starts from the top down. Executives must champion the efforts and lead by example. This can mean articulating employee well-being as a company value, including employee safety as a business priority, and visibly engaging in those efforts.

At an Atlanta nonprofit, healthy eating and accommodating dietary needs has become part of the culture. Chris, the head of HR, invited an employee with allergies to corn, eggs and yeast to sit on the planning committee for employee events.

Jen, who is on a doctor-recommended gluten-free diet, wasn't so lucky. One day when everyone was in the lunch room except Jen, the CEO shared an article she had read about gluten and how "these people that say they have a gluten issue are just looking for attention."

Most everyone in her office knows Jen is gluten-free, so a coworker (also on a doctor-recommended gluten-free diet) tried to explain that there are a lot of gluten-sensitivity issues that are not always true allergies. The CEO turned a deaf ear. When Jen walked into the room shortly thereafter with her lunch, the CEO snickered and rolled her eyes.

Over the next several years, the CEO made other comments like "What weird thing is Jen eating today?" or "Well, if Jen made this, there has to be something weird with it." She would even question Jen's ability to do her job when holding menu tastings for the annual gala: "How can you be doing your job if you can't taste the food?" Jen explained that she asks the CEO and donors to attend tastings so they can provide insight on the menu items and flavors they would enjoy.

Employers must remove barriers that prevent employees from experiencing a safe and inclusive workplace. Some measures should be adopted to make healthy choices easier for employees to make. Company policies, from recruitment to retirement, that should support employee well-being through food safety, and incorporate the dietary needs of employees, include:

Food Environments

- Label menu items with allergens. In the cafeteria and at meetings, list nutrition information as well as if any of the top eight allergens (wheat, soy, egg, milk, tree nuts, peanuts, fish, shellfish) or other ingredients avoided by employees (e.g., pork). Also label if items are vegan, vegetarian, gluten-free, kosher or halal.
- Ensure food safety procedures are adhered to in the cafeteria. Verify that your food service providers follow state and federal guidelines when storing, preparing and serving food to employees as well as when cleaning food preparation and serving areas.
- Offer healthier and/or more accommodating options in vending machines. Inquire about adding prepackaged kosher, vegan and vegetarian options. Offer a mix of traditional treats and healthier choices. Price the healthier options lower than the traditional options to encourage healthy choices.
- Institute food-safety guidelines for employee kitchens. Employee kitchens are full of landmines for food-allergic employees. From toaster ovens to the refrigerator, countertops to microwaves, traces of other people's meals linger in shared equipment. Ensure employees wrap food cooked in the microwave with a paper towel, not only to keep their food from contaminating the microwave, but also to avoid contaminants in the microwave from dripping into their food. Provide separate prep areas and/or equipment for only food-allergic employees to use, e.g. gluten-free toasters. Designate areas in shared refrigerators for these employees to place their food.

Company Practices

Equally important are the company's practices to support employee well-being and belonging.

- Teach employees about dietary needs. Incorporate lunch-and-learns into your wellness program on different dietary needs: veganism, celiac disease, kosher diets, and food allergies. Allow employees to teach them so they can give insight into their food world. When people learn from each other, it opens up dialogue and brings about understanding about another's way of life.

- Meetings and Events. Do staff meetings offer food and beverage that everyone can enjoy? Are employees given the opportunity to provide their dietary needs when registering for the holiday party or incentive trip? Are employee potlucks inclusive and are dishes labeled with ingredients? Practices that are consistent with a company's well-being initiatives can go a long way towards establishing a healthy, safe and inclusive culture.
- Recruiting. While you legally cannot ask someone if they have food allergies or follow a religious based diet during the recruitment process, you can give them information on your corporate culture around food and beverage. Share that you provide inclusive menus for all employees, the cafeteria has signs with nutritional information and allergens, and food safety policies are posted in employee kitchens. Even those without special dietary needs will likely appreciate such inclusiveness and consideration.

One final note: Workplace accommodations for people with visible or invisible disabilities (dietary needs) are actually about managing effectively rather than making exceptions. It's about having clear expectations, open communication, and inclusive practices. In the end, when employers create an environment that emphasizes employee well-being, authenticity and inclusiveness, employees feel supported. And healthier, happier employees increase engagement with company goals, tie their well-being to their professional success, and provide a competitive advantage to employers.

ABOUT THE AUTHOR
Tracy Stuckrath
CSEP, CMM, CHC, CFPM

Tracy Stuckrath is the President and Chief Food Officer of **Thrive!**

Tracy has over 25 years' experience planning meetings and events—for two Olympic games, consumer and trade magazines, and private corporations and associations. She speaks regularly at events worldwide to share insight on creating safe, inclusive food and beverage events.

Tracy realized later in life the importance food has to both health and relationships. As one of 15 million Americans with food allergies, she has both personal and professional experience in managing dietary needs at events.

Tracy holds a number of food-related certifications, such as ServSafe® Allergen Training and Beyond Celiac gluten-free training. She is also designated a Certified Special Events Professional, Certified Meetings Manager, Certified Health Coach, and Certified Food Protection Manager.

In addition to serving on the Slow Food Atlanta Board of Directors, she has served as the chair of the FARE Walk for Food Allergy Atlanta since 2012. She also chaired the Allie Awards in 2010 and 2015, and she was selected to join Les Dames d'Escoffier in 2016.

Tracy is a graduate of NC State University. She's a fan of NC State football, the Dallas Cowboys, and the Baltimore Orioles. In her spare time, she enjoys gardening, exercising, and taking her nephew and nieces on adventures.

EMAIL tracy@thrivemeetings.com
PHONE (404) 242-0530
WEBSITE www.thrivefoodmatters.com
WEBSITE www.tracystuckrath.com
LINKEDIN /in/tracystuckrath
FACEBOOK /thrivemeetingsevents
TWITTER @tstuckrath

Shelly Trent

What You Have to Lose:
The Costs of Internal Career Development

Engaging employees. Recruiting the best talent. Retaining institutional knowledge. Planning for mass retirements. These topics are on the minds of human resources professionals across the globe.

So what is the key to winning the talent war? An internal career development program. How do I know? Because I have implemented such programs. Let me share with you the "why," the "how," and the "how much."

Let's start with the "why." Randstad US conducted the Employer Branding Survey in 2015, which showed that the top reason why employees leave jobs is "lack of a career path." The study revealed that employees who had left their jobs in the past year cited a lack of career development opportunities (26 percent) as the prime reason for leaving their organizations. Companies, then, can promote their training and development initiatives as a way to recruit and retain talent.

The Association for Talent Development (ATD) published a State of the Industry Report in 2014, which showed that organizations with fewer than 500 employees spend a little over $1,200 per person on internal career development programs. Organizations with over 500 employees are likely to spend over $1,800 per person.

While that may seem like a large amount of money at first glance, consider how much your other benefits cost. The Employer Health Benefits Survey, conducted by the Kaiser Family Foundation and the Health Research & Educational Trust in 2016, showed that, on average, employers pay about $12,600 per employee for health benefits. With that in mind, $1,200 to $1,800 per employee for development spending doesn't seem so expensive in comparison.

Before you say *but it will cost too much*, consider the cost of *not* providing employee development benefits. Although the recession of 2008-2009 brought an employer's (or buyer's) market, it has turned now into a job seeker's (or seller's) market. In 2017, and going forward into the next several years at least, it is likely to continue to be a seller's market, meaning that the job seekers will be selective and discriminating in their acceptance of job offers. They will be seeking positions that not only pay well, but also that offer excellent benefits, including training and development.

In 2012, Deloitte Consulting surveyed 560 employees across every job function and type of organization, and established the following:

- Employees who planned to change companies cited a lack of career progression as the top factor, over compensation.
- Employees are more likely to stay with their organization if their skills are being used effectively and they feel challenged by the work.
- Employees who are part of a succession plan or who work for an organization that promotes from within are less likely to leave.
- Beyond succession planning, companies should focus specific retention strategies on high-potential employees to ensure their talents are being used to the fullest extent.
- Employees who have been with their companies for fewer than two years or who are Millennials are more likely to leave than older employees who have been with the organization longer.
- Organizations should specifically tailor their strategies for engaging, developing, and retaining employees to the four generations in the workplace.

When a potential hire refuses your job offer, do you ask why? Many studies show that the main reasons job seekers turn down opportunities are a lack of the following: professional development, promotional opportunities, work-life balance, pay, health benefits, and corporate culture. Health benefits and salary will be a large expense for your company, and professional development less so, but promotional opportunities, work-life balance, and culture don't really cost much, if anything. The internal career development prospects, next to pay and health benefits, are likely the most important issues for job seekers.

For the last ten years, human resources professionals have focused on employee engagement as one of the key issues they face. In the Randstad study mentioned above, it was found that although CEOs realize the value of employee development, they do not allocate appropriate resources for this purpose. If your organization truly aims to engage current employees and recruit top talent, you need to convince your C-suite of the value of this critical employee benefit. To do this, you will need to bring to your organization's leaders data about cost to replace—which, according to the Bliss-Gately tool, is 1.5 times the position's salary. So, if you hire someone who earns $50,000, and that person leaves after three years, you will spend $75,000 to refill that role, when you include the cost and time to recruit and train someone else. Given that fact, don't you think your CEO would say that using employee career development programs internally to recruit great talent and retain those workers is well worth the investment?

According to a CompData benchmarking survey, the U.S. turnover rate for 2016 was 18.1 percent, up from 15.6 percent in 2014. What is your turnover rate? Let's say it's 16 percent. If your organization employs 500 workers, with an average salary of $50,000, and has a 16 percent turnover rate, turnover is actually costing your organization about $6 million a year (based on the cost-to-replace calculation tool). When you look at data like this, internal employee development programs that cost around $1200-$1800 per person seem like a steal!

Now you may be asking yourself how *your* organization can create and implement an internal career development program that will allow *you* to recruit top talent, engage your employees, retain staff, and therefore lower turnover. I was hired to do just that by a former employer, so I will share with you the elements of such a program.

The first task I undertook was to review and update all job descriptions in the organization. Rather than simply have employees review their current descriptions and acknowledge that it represented their work, my team and I instead had them consider not only their day-to-day duties, but also the competencies and soft skills associated with their jobs. We asked them to consider whether the job actually should require a certain level of education or training, and what skills were needed to be successful. We used a competency tool to aid them in determining the most critical competencies needed for the job. This proved especially important for those at the director level and above, where a higher level of emotional intelligence and soft skills are vital. I worked with staff at all levels of the organization, performing job analyses to ensure that the job descriptions were as accurate as possible. The reason for undertaking this as the first step will become apparent shortly.

After the job analyses were completed, we made them available to employees so they could consider whether they might be interested in a different role in the organization. Our CEO was quite forward-thinking and realized that the key to low turnover was keeping employees engaged and challenged to do more and advance themselves while also advancing the mission of the organization. One key area he felt should be addressed was internal promotional opportunities. The CEO encouraged the organizational leaders to promote from within, but that was not happening as often as he would have liked. He tasked me with investigating the reasons why.

I researched the positions that had been filled over the last six months and interviewed the hiring managers. What I found was surprising. I expected to find that internal employees did not have the work experience needed to secure a different position. Instead, I found that employees were not preparing for interviews because they assumed that if the organization valued internal promotion, they didn't have to put forth the same level of effort as an external candidate. Many of the employees had been in their jobs for years and had not been on interviews for some time. Therefore, our employees were providing outdated resumes, dressing too casually for the interview, arriving unprepared to answer interview questions, and learning little about the position they sought.

One of the next initiatives for our newly launched employee development program was to educate our internal candidates on the interview process. We held several one-day seminars for staff on resume writing, dressing for the interview, researching the position and department, crafting responses to behavioral interview questions, and following up with thank you notes to the hiring manager. Following that training, we saw the number of internal promotions rise. Hiring managers were very pleased with the quality of internal candidates who were able to compete.

At the same time that we were holding these programs to teach employees how to obtain a promotion, we developed a year-long leadership development program. Our first group of employees to go through the program were current supervisors. Even the chief officers participated in order to show other leaders the significance of attending. This year-long, once-a-month program consisted of day or half-day sessions on topics such as performance management, coaching, supervisory skills, employment law, diversity, team building, and more. Once the current supervisory staff had completed the program, we opened it up for a second round to employees who aspired to be in such a position in the future. This allowed us to develop potential leaders from within and ensure their readiness to take on additional responsibilities. We trained employees in exactly what we wanted them to know, rather than leave it to them to find their own developmental opportunities.

Another component of our internal employee career development program was creating individual development plans (IDPs) for each staff member, from the front-desk receptionist to the CEO. The goal was to find out what employees' backgrounds and education were, whether they were a good fit for their current job or may be a better fit for another role, whether they were interested in participating in a succession plan, and so on. I gathered information from each employee regarding their prior education, training, and work experience. We also had each person complete a self-assessment tool that provided the following results regarding their current positions:

- Move up (vertical) – interested in promotional opportunities
- Move down (realignment) – wants less responsibility or no longer desires supervisory role
- Move out (relocation) – may be ready to leave the organization altogether
- Move across (lateral) – wishes to stay with the organization, but in a different position at the same level

- Grow in place (enrichment) – enjoys current job, and wants to increase skill level for role
- Investigating possibilities (exploration) – wants to stay with the organization, but wants to learn something new

Once employees had completed the assessment, I met with each person to create a personalized plan for their development. Employees had the option to have two plans: one to share with their supervisor and one that would be kept confidential. The reason for this? Some employees did not want their supervisors to know that they might be considering a new role or a different department. Although the CEO strongly encouraged supervisors to coach employees to grow and develop, some staff members were uncomfortable sharing their goals of leaving their current position. In those cases, I worked with employees to create one IDP to set goals for their current role that could be shared with their supervisors, and another IDP where I would work with them on development opportunities to prepare them for their next position.

Let's look at two examples of how this process was successful for the organization. One young woman worked in the collections department. She liked the corporate culture and, in general, enjoyed working for the organization because of its mission and reputation, though she didn't feel that she was using her strengths. It was "just a job" in a good company. Upon interviewing her about her past experience and education, I discovered that her background was in graphic design and writing. It just so happened that I knew that the woman who was responsible for the corporate newsletter, internal and external publications, and design was considering early retirement due to health issues. I went to the chief officers and pled my case: we need to create a role for this young woman to work alongside the current publications manager to prepare her for the role. All agreed that this would benefit the organization, so for about nine to twelve months, there were two people in the publications office until the manager retired. This was obviously a win-win: the young woman was able to use her talents and the organization was able to retain a good employee. She is is now the director of the publications department, leading other staff.

A second example is that one of the employee's assessments showed that he was thinking of leaving the organization to return to the field of hotel management. He had lived in Atlanta in the past, and was considering moving back. I assisted him in reworking his resume and coached him on changing careers. You might ask, "Why would an organization spend time helping someone leave?" My answer is, "Why not?" If they are unhappy, they may not be producing above-average work. Want positive comments about your workplace on Glassdoor.com? Want referrals from past employees? This is one way to make that happen! After this young man secured a hotel job in Atlanta, I happened to be in the area and met him for dinner. He had been working in Atlanta for about nine months by this time. At dinner, he shared with me that the "grass was not always greener on the other side," and that he had made a mistake. He said he didn't realize how much he really enjoyed his former job and the culture of the organization. He asked if I could help him return to his prior role. He had been a stellar employee, so we welcomed him back. He is still working at the organization and has been there for over twenty years total. He was not the only former employee who returned after leaving for a short time.

To further develop our leadership/supervisory training program, we created a corporate university. We held half- and whole-day sessions on the work of each department to educate employees on how their roles contributed to the mission of the organization. Following the sessions, employees understood how their skills could be used by other departments, which would then allow staff to determine if they wanted to change jobs. Since all the job descriptions were up to date and available for review, employees could learn what skills, education, and competencies were needed to successfully transition internally. Once an employee had determined which jobs he was interested in pursuing, we could create an IDP to prepare him for the role. For example, if the potential future job required a degree, but the employee had not yet finished college, the IDP would reflect the employee's need and desire to finish school. In that case, I would assist him with applying to college, selecting courses, and securing tuition reimbursement. Knowing that the organization was investing in his future would ensure that the employee would most likely be engaged and retained for the long term.

To assist employees in returning to complete or start their college education, we held "lunch and learn" sessions where representatives from area universities visited the organization to answer employee questions about degree programs, admissions, and more. The organization provided tuition assistance, and so employees were encouraged to attend college classes.

The next stage of the internal employee development program was to establish a succession plan. The chief officers determined that because they encouraged internal promotion, a formal succession plan would create a career path that would not only prepare employees for future roles, but would also retain the best talent, as staff members knew that the organization was investing in their career progression.

As mentioned earlier, the job descriptions had been updated to include competencies, so this accelerated the process of developing a succession plan. Rather than have the organizational leaders hand select those who would participate in the succession plan, we allowed employees to opt in if they were interested in being considered for future positions. We wanted to be transparent and allow all employees to feel empowered to participate.

In addition to the ongoing employee development and leadership training, staff members could review the job descriptions for the positions they might eventually fill. This allowed them to understand what could be expected of them in the future, and to plan for their professional development in a targeted way.

For employees who wanted to prepare for a specific position in the C-suite, the chief officers worked directly with those staff members to mentor them, answer questions, and determine the readiness of those in the pipeline. To do this, we used assessment centers to observe the candidates in a variety of situations. Small groups of employees who were preparing for eventual c-suite positions were provided with real-life scenarios of incidents and events which occurred or could potentially occur in the roles they were seeking, or other activities they would be expected to perform in a higher-level role. Examples of this included presenting at conferences, speaking to the media, and completing special projects. This would enable the c-suite to observe those in the line of succession in behavioral situations using the necessary competencies.

Another advantage that follows from succession planning is the transfer of institutional knowledge. With the coming mass retirements of baby boomers in your workforce, this is an issue you will undoubtedly face. When employees retire, they take with them not only the work they performed on a daily basis, but also the knowledge, competencies, and connections they made on the job.

Here is an example: Let's say you have an older male sales representative who has hundreds of satisfied long-term clients. He has brought in many new accounts due to his ability to build relationships and serve his clients with swiftness and ease, brought about by his familiarity with your products and his clients' needs. He's been in that role for twenty years, and plans to retire in two years. If this person were your employee, would you hire someone now, two years before your star sales representative retires, or wait to replace him after retirement? If you're thinking ahead, you'd bring someone in or promote someone internally to shadow him for two years.

Why? You might be thinking that this will cost your organization two years of salary for someone to have an extended orientation. However, that viewpoint is shortsighted. In those two years, the retiring sales representative could introduce the new employee to his clients, help build strong relationships, and pave the way for the ensured success of his replacement, thereby sharing twenty years of institutional knowledge. Those two years are an important and invaluable investment in your organization's success. If you decide to wait until the sales representative retires *before* hiring a replacement, it may take more than two years for the new salesperson to build strong connections. Relationships are not inevitable just because a new person is hired to take over a sales account. Clients who were loyal to the former salesperson may not have a positive relationship with the new hire, or it may take clients a while to build trust. Your organization could lose business!

Furthermore, let's assume that the retiring sales representative, due to his long tenure in your organization, is earning a salary of $100,000. If you decide to hire someone for less, supposing that he or she may be younger, you might only offer a salary of $50,000. You might think you are saving your company $50,000 a year. However, if the new hire doesn't retain the accounts due to relationship management issues, your organization will lose money. Likewise, if the new employee doesn't stay in the job more than two or three years, it will cost 1.5 times his or her salary to replace the position, and each new hire after that, since younger employees tend to change jobs every two to three years. It would be an advantage to have someone shadowing the retiring salesman for two years, and since the organization is showing an investment in the incoming salesperson, it is more likely that he or she will remain in the organization longer.

Another aspect of our employee development program was departmental team building. In order to reward and recognize employees in a meaningful way, I held team-building sessions with each department where I had employees select their top three recognition methods from a list of items. Choices included verbal praise in front of other employees, a day off, a certificate of recognition, a thank you letter, lunch with their boss, a gift certificate, etc. The department head then knew how to show appreciation to employees in a personal way, rather than giving employees the same reward. We also had each department take the Myers-Briggs Type Indicator, and I worked with each group to explain and showcase the strengths of each staff member. We also talked about how different types work best, how they can communicate with each other more effectively, and how others perceive them.

In addition to all the other employee development activities mentioned in this article, we also made our corporate culture one of constant appreciation. Other activities included:

- Business casual dress and casual Friday. We worked with a vendor to create corporate logo wear, so that if someone did not have an important meeting that day, he or she was allowed to wear khakis and a logo shirt in lieu of business casual. Summers were all casual unless we were attending off-site meetings or hosting a meeting.
- Time off to volunteer. We allowed up to three days of paid time off if an employee provided proof that he or she was volunteering at an organization related to our mission.
- Flex days. Employees could work their hours over a period of two weeks and take one day off every other week.
- Secret pals. It might sound corny, but it was fun. Anyone who chose to participate drew names and for the next year, employees did something each month for their "pal," such as a small gift, flowers, a card, treats, etc.

- Charity silent auctions. Twice a year, we held a silent auction for all staff where the funds raised went to support a nonprofit organization with a similar mission. Employees brought in items for the auction such as desserts, artwork, and home décor items.

As you can see, there are a variety of methods to develop employees in meaningful ways that don't cost as much as you might guess. Our employees knew we valued them because we showed it through numerous activities. Our turnover rate was around one percent, and even when employees left, some of them returned within a year. Victor Lipman, a Harvard-educated author, executive coach, and trainer said in *Forbes*, "Loyal employees are more engaged. Engaged employees are more productive." Gallup polls estimate that disengaged employees cost U.S. employers between $450 billion and $550 billion per year in productivity, not to mention the cost of replacement.

As human resources professionals, we spend a majority of our time dealing with daily issues as they occur, rather than planning for the future of our organizations. We need to make time for the engagement and development of our employees. Consider hiring a staff member whose sole role is to make your workplace one of recognition, engagement, and personal and professional development. You will need to convince your C-suite of the value of this position, but I assure you that an extra FTE in HR will, in the long term, save you possibly millions of dollars in turnover and disengaged employees.

Shelly Trent

SPHR, SHRM-SCP, CAE

Shelly Trent is a career coach, writer, speaker, and educator in Human Resources. She has more than 16 years' experience working for the Society of Human Resource Management (SHRM).

Aside from human resources, Shelly's background includes university continuing education, college career services, and business and industry training. She has served as an adjunct faculty member at Indiana University Southeast's School of Business, where she taught business students about career planning and job searching. She was also associate editor of the National Career Development Association's *Career Convergence* magazine for three years.

Shelly is a specialist in adult career development. She has completed her Ph.D. coursework (all but dissertation) in HRD/OD and career counseling.

Shelly is married with two cats and one dog—all rescues. In her free time, she enjoys weather (she's a certified storm spotter) and collecting Beatles' memorabilia. Her Myers-Briggs type is INFJ.

EMAIL shellytrent@live.com
PHONE (502) 235-6438
LINKEDIN /in/shellytrent
TWITTER @HRDShelly